Home Library

Caring for Your Child

Manufactured in the United States of America

ISBN: 0-88176-369-1

Illustrations: Nan Brooks
Cover Design: Michael Johnson

CONTENTS

Introduction 3
The Parent/Physician
   Partnership 6
Fever 8
The Pediatric Medicine Chest . . . 10
Administering Medication 12
Immunizations 14
Caring for Your Child 16
Index 153

NOTICE

In this book, the authors and editors have done their best to outline the indicated general treatment for various childhood conditions, diseases, ailments, and their symptoms. Also, recommendations are made regarding certain drugs, medications, and preparations.

Different people react to the same treatment, medication, or preparation in different ways. This book does not purport to answer all questions about all situations that you or your child may encounter. It does not attempt to replace your physician.

Neither the editors nor the publisher of this book takes responsibility for any possible consequences from any treatment, action, or application of medication or preparation to any child by any person reading or following the information or advice contained in this book. The publication of this book does not constitute the practice of medicine. The author and publisher advise that you consult your physician before administering any medication or undertaking any course of treatment.

INTRODUCTION

Childhood illnesses can be perplexing to a distraught parent. The infant's first sniffle, an unexplained rash, the newborn's colicky distress, all can make a parent anxious not only to relieve the child's discomfort but also to make sure that the ailment is not a signal of serious illness. Does the child's fever indicate a sore throat, infectious mononucleosis, or a myriad of other diseases in which fever is present?

A minor cut can easily be diagnosed by the parent, and it can be dealt with appropriately without hesitation. But if the child has a serious fall and injures his arm, how can the parent tell if it's a fracture? If the child is hit on the head with a ball, could he have a concussion? If a burn is more than minor, can the parent treat it, or should the child be taken to a health care facility?

Such questions can cause the anxious parent serious concern, sometimes even panic. CARING FOR YOUR CHILD urges parents to plan ahead for ailments that can and do occur at any time. Some problems can be treated at home; others demand a doctor's care. The informed parent has a far better chance of promptly identifying which is which than does one who is unprepared. It is difficult to second guess what a child may get into that will cause an injury, which viruses he may be exposed to, when he will come down with a bad sore throat. The parent who can consult CARING FOR YOUR CHILD will know what symptoms to look for to judge the severity of a cough, what he can do at home to comfort the child, when he must consult a doctor.

continued

3

Each profile covers a single disease or condition and includes a description that will aid the parent in identifying the probable cause of the problem. The parent will find the descriptions helpful in distinguishing impetigo from ringworm, colic from teething pains. Each description is written to reassure the parent if the condition tends to be self-correcting, or to alert the parent if serious complications are possible.

How is the diagnosis for a single disease confirmed? You'll find out if you can diagnose the problem at home, if it must be done in the doctor's office, or if laboratory tests or screenings are necessary.

If home treatment is possible or helpful, CARING FOR YOUR CHILD tells you what you can do: how to make your child more comfortable when he has a cold, the emergency measures necessary if he has swallowed poison or is choking on a bone. The Home Treatment section of each entry also describes the home therapy your doctor may prescribe—a course of drugs or a special diet.

Precautions that should be taken to protect your child are also included. The precautions will not only help to prevent your child from getting ill, but will also alert you to possible complications, drug misuse, and those situations in which you must see the doctor.

The Doctor's Treatment section of each entry is not a recommended treatment but rather an overall view of what your doctor might find necessary—including laboratory tests, X rays, drug therapy, hospitalization, and surgery. Reading this section will prepare you by letting you know what to expect from your office visit.

By reading these entries, you can become familiar with what you can do to avoid serious illness and when you must seek medical aid. As a home medical text, CARING FOR YOUR CHILD will also guide you in those steps that should *not* be taken.

CARING FOR YOUR CHILD will guide you in making decisions about medical care—it explains how to choose the best doctor for your child, and what you should keep in your home medicine chest. A chapter tells which immu-

nizations are necessary, at what age they should be administered, and whether boosters are necessary to provide your child lifelong protection.

CARING FOR YOUR CHILD tells you how to give the proper amount of medication to a child, what "four times a day" means, and why it's important that you continue treatment for as long as the doctor prescribes, even if your child's symptoms clear up earlier.

CARING FOR YOUR CHILD is written in easy to understand language. You'll find it a reliable aid in helping to decide whether to call the doctor, go to the emergency room, or treat the child at home. Of course, you must consult your doctor about drug usage or any unusual symptoms your child has.

Take an hour or so to browse through this book before a specific need arises. You want to know beforehand how to deal with an emergency situation such as choking or poisoning. And you want to be alert to those early warning symptoms that may indicate serious illness. By taking the time to become familiar with this book, you will be able to use the information contained herein wisely and well when it's needed.

Children do get sick. They fall and cut themselves; they pick up germs; they suffer from allergies, and headaches, and bumps and pains. Every parent wants to be able to help his child feel better faster and to guard him from serious illness. CARING FOR YOUR CHILD can be a real tool for every parent.

THE PARENT/ PHYSICIAN PARTNERSHIP

Raising a child properly to good emotional and physical health is a tough job that requires cooperation and love from all the child's guardians. A trained and experienced person, who is a reliable and sympathetic source of information and suggestions, can help immeasurably. Your child's doctor should be that person. But he or she should not take the child's rearing out of your hands by making all decisions for you or by dictating a single course of action without adequate explanation. Only you, the parent, can make judgments concerning what is best for your child—judgments based on knowing the important facts and alternatives. Above all else, you should feel comfortable talking to your child's doctor and following his or her advice.

Whom to Choose. To get the best from your child's doctor, you must first select the best doctor for your child. A pediatrician sees only children and has had three to five years post-doctoral training in the special emotional, physical, and educational needs of young people. A family physician usually has had nearly as much training, but it has not been devoted exclusively to children. The best pediatrician in the country should know more about children than the best family doctor, but neither will know everything about all children. A family doctor who is interested in children—in your child in particular—and with whom you feel safe and comfortable may be a better choice for you than a pediatrician with whom you can't relate.

There are several ways to go about finding a physician for your family. If you are an expectant mother, your obstetrician can recommend a number of local pediatricians and family physicians from which to choose. If you are new to an area you may consult a neighbor who has children or call the local hospital or branch of the state medical society. An initial phone call and visit to a doctor should determine whether or not that physician is right for you and your child. Once you find a doctor with whom you feel confident, there are a number of ways you can help promote your child's good care.

Take Time to Make Time. A common cause of communication breakdown between parent and physician is the complaint: "My doctor didn't give me enough time to ask all my questions!" This conflict can be avoided if, when you make an appointment, you let the receptionist know what the visit is for and that you will need extra time to discuss this (or another) problem with the doctor. If possible, you should mention your problems in advance so the doctor can consider them before seeing your child. A hurried doctor might be tempted to offer you brief, off-the-cuff advice to ease your mind and to keep up with his schedule, but this approach leaves you cheated and the doctor feeling guilty. Allow your doctor time to treat one thing at a time.

With rare exception, children's doctors are glad to allow time to discuss complicated problems... *if* they are forewarned. If you feel rushed during your appointment, simply request time to discuss the situation or ask to come back when more time is available.

Ask Questions. If a doctor's advice seems wrong to you or is hard to follow, ask "Why?" and "What are the alternatives?" If you don't like the answers, try another doctor, but don't argue. You may get what you want, but it may be second- or third-best for your child.

Before You Call. Be prepared to answer questions when you phone your doctor for advice. You will get much better service if you have the following at the tip of your tongue:

- your child's approximate weight (medications are given by weight);
- your child's temperature (take it by thermometer; don't guess);
- what medicines the child is allergic to;
- what illnesses the child has been exposed to recently; and
- the druggist's name and telephone number and the hours the pharmacy is open (days, nights, weekends, and holidays).

Finally, have paper and pencil at hand to write down any instructions the doctor might give you.

Health Forms. Before submitting camp and school forms and health insurance claims, fill in whatever is required on your part and as much other information as you can. Grant your doctor time to practice his profession, not his penmanship.

A Second Opinion. If you want another doctor's opinion, ask for a consultation. No physician relishes assuming all the responsibility for a difficult case. Allow the doctor you trust to suggest the names of possible consultants. You can trust the competence of the consultant as you do your own doctor's.

Satisfaction Guaranteed. Let your doctor know when you are displeased with the service you are receiving. If it can be changed to better suit your needs, it will be. If not, find another physician.

As there are good and bad lawyers, engineers, teachers, and parents, there are also good and bad doctors. But a physician's failure to please you may be due to many factors other than professional inadequacy. To ensure a good relationship and the best possible care for your child, select your doctor carefully and communicate openly. Your child's good health care depends on your physician and you.

FEVER

There is a popular fallacy that says that the higher the fever, the sicker the child. It is also believed that fever is a child's enemy, that it should be fought and the temperature brought to normal.

The fact is that children past early infancy tend to develop high fevers with little provocation. Relatively harmless illnesses like roseola often cause temperatures as high as 106°F, whereas many lethal diseases, such as leukemia and polio, may cause slight or no temperature deviations at all.

A child is as seriously sick as the illness warrants, not as a thermometer registers. A child with pneumonia or meningitis and a fever of 104°F is still as ill after the temperature is artificially reduced to normal. A child with a strep throat and 101°F fever is no less threatened than the same child with a strep throat and a temperature of 104°F. Prostration, disorientation, difficulty in breathing, and other symptoms are means to decide the illness's severity, not the degree of fever.

Fever: Friend and Foe. You should first regard a fever as a child's friend rather than an enemy. A fever is an early warning signal that a child is ill and that you must look to find a cause. It is also a helpful barometer to judge, together with other symptoms, when an illness is ending. The course of a fever indicates whether or not an antibiotic is working effectively. It speeds up the body's metabolic processes (possibly including its immunizing mechanisms) and in some instances may help the body's defenses to overcome an illness. Finally, the pattern of daily fluctuations in a fever may be characteristic of particular illnesses and aid in making a correct diagnosis.

A high fever does have disadvantages, however. It makes a child feel bad and, as it develops, causes chills. If a fever continues for days, it will debilitate a child and cause weakness and the need for a longer recuperation period. In susceptible younger children a fever may precipitate convulsions. For all these reasons, it is sensible to reduce a fever. But it is important not to confuse treating the fever with treating the illness and not to panic as a fever rises or to harm the child in your anxiety to fight the fever.

A Matter of Degree. At any given moment, different parts of the body are at different temperatures. Moreover, normal temperatures vary as much as two to three degrees Fahrenheit over the course of a day even when a child is healthy. A rectal temperature of 99.8°F or less, an oral temperature of 98.6°F or below, and an armpit temperature, though the least accurate, of 98°F or less are all considered normal.

Despite these variances, all thermometers are marked to indicate 98.6°F as normal. A rectal thermometer differs from an oral one only in having a more rugged bulb. (The most practical instrument for home use is a stubby bulb thermometer, which can be used to take a child's temperature either orally or rectally.)

Any type of thermometer—rectal, stubby, or oral—can be used to take a rectal temperature. If the oral one is pressed into service, extra care must be taken because of its more pointed and fragile bulb. For the most reliable readings at any age, the rectal thermometer is recommended, although it takes a bit more time for a fever to register.

Taking the Temperature. No one can estimate the degree of a fever by touch, not even a mother. If your child feels warm or appears ill, you must use a thermometer to attain the information you and your doctor need to treat the child.

Read the thermometer before inserting it to be certain the mercury column is below 98.6°F and the bulb is intact. Spread the child's buttocks widely enough with the thumb and forefinger of one hand so the anal opening is clearly visible. Lubricate the bulb and insert it gently into the center of the anus. There should be no pain or discomfort. (Only the bulb portion of the thermometer needs to be inserted for the two to three minutes required to obtain an accurate reading.)

You can sufficiently restrain a baby by placing him or her face down on a solid surface and putting the heel of your hand firmly on the lower back. An uncooperative toddler can be firmly clasped between your thighs and bent forward over one leg in a position to expose the target.

Although less reliable, an oral reading will suffice and can be taken in a child who is old enough to hold the bulb of the thermometer under the tongue for three minutes.

Care of Your Thermometer. After each use, the thermometer should be shaken down below "normal" and washed with soap and cold water. To sterilize it, you may soak the thermometer in an alcohol solution before storing it in its case. Place it back in the medicine cabinet where it will be handy the next time you need it.

Treatment of Fever. The most reliable medications for lowering fever are aspirin and acetaminophen. Due to recent research possibly linking Reye's syndrome with the use of aspirin in children, it is recommended that you consult your doctor before administering aspirin to reduce a fever. Sixty milligrams of either aspirin or acetaminophen may be given for every 12 pounds of the child's weight and repeated every four hours if necessary. This formula works out to one children's aspirin for every 15 pounds of weight. Keep a feverish child lightly clothed or covered to allow the body heat to escape, and give plenty of liquids.

THE PEDIATRIC MEDICINE CHEST

The contents of a medicine chest may be as simple or as elaborate as the special needs of your child and the availability of professional medical services. Be sure to consult your doctor before purchasing and administering any medications. In average circumstances, the following list of items should meet all your needs in semi-emergency situations until you can reach your pharmacy. All items should be clearly labeled in their original containers with child-proof tops and should be stored out of reach of even the most inquisitive young child.

RECOMMENDED CONTENTS:
acetaminophen
adhesive bandages (assorted sizes)
adhesive tape
antiseptic solution
aspirin
burn ointment
cough medicine
decongestant
emetic
knitted roller bandage
lubricant
nasal aspirator
sterile gauze pads
steristrips
steroids
syrup of ipecac
thermometer

ASPIRIN AND ACETAMINOPHEN
Aspirin and acetaminophen are used to relieve pain and fever. Both are available as flavored, chewable tablets and adult tablets, as rectal suppositories, and in various strengths. Suppository forms are useful when a child is vomiting. These should be stored in a refrigerator to prevent melting. Aspirin may be crushed and mixed with a spoonful of applesauce, jelly, or ice cream. Acetaminophen also comes as drops and syrup. **Caution:** The strengths of the popular brands differ; check the label. Be aware of the different strengths and administer only in recommended dosages. Recent research has shown a possible link between the use of aspirin in children and Reye's syndrome. Consult your doctor before using aspirin.

COUGH MEDICINE
Cough medicine should be kept on hand to suppress a severe night cough. **Caution:** A suppressant cough medicine should never be given to a child who has croup or any type of hindered breathing.

EMETIC
This medicine induces vomiting in cases of swallowed poison. It should be in every medicine chest. Syrup of ipecac is recommended. Before using an emetic, verify that inducing vomiting is the appropriate treatment for the specific poison by contacting a Poison Control Center. Keep the phone number in your medicine chest and by your phone.

STEROIDS
Steroids are helpful in cases of hives, hay fever, croup, reactions to insect bites, sun poisoning, poison ivy, and asthma, but they must be used cautiously. Discuss with your doctor the advisability of keeping a few doses of a liquid, tablet, or topical steroid on hand.

THERMOMETER AND LUBRICANT
A multipurpose, stubby-bulb thermometer is most practical. Any lubricating ointment will serve to grease a thermometer for rectal use, but a water-soluble gel is superior because it readily washes off in cold water.

ADDITIONS
Antiseptic solution, burn ointment, sterile gauze pads (2×2 and 3×3 inches), rolls of knitted bandage (2-inch and 3-inch), adhesive tape ($\frac{1}{4}$ inch), steristrips, and adhesive bandages of assorted sizes are all useful in treating minor accidents properly.

ADMINISTERING MEDICATION

When a proper diagnosis has been made and the most appropriate medicine selected, the child's physician is home free. But the third, and often most decisive, factor in the child's health care is the parent's responsibility to administer the medicine correctly. Ten to thirty percent of treatment failures are directly due to inadequate administration of an effective drug. If the doctor's directions are vague, or you don't understand them, ask for clarification.

DOSAGE

Most medications are prescribed in proportion to a child's weight. Accurate liquid measurements are important. "One teaspoonful" does not mean any old teaspoon. It means one measuring teaspoonful, or 5.0 cubic-centimeters (cc). "One-half teaspoonful" does not mean guessing when an ordinary spoon is half full. It means 2.5 cc, or a full half-teaspoon measuring spoon. Ask your pharmacist to recommend a medicine dropper or spoon that will make it easy to accurately measure and administer liquid medication.

TIMING

"Four times a day" means that four doses should be given within every 24 hours, but the child's sleep doesn't need to be interrupted. The four doses should be spread out as widely as is possible and convenient while the child is awake. "Every six hours" means just that: one dose is given every six hours around the clock.

DURATION

Most relapses and many complications are the result of stopping medication prematurely. Often a child feels and acts well before he is well. Earaches stop, fevers vanish, coughs subside, and appetites return when germs are merely stunned and healing is scarcely begun. Strep infections require 10 or more days of antibiotic therapy before the infection is gone. Urinary tract infections and ear infections often take even longer to cure, although symptoms may disappear in a day. So be sure you continue any medication for as long as it has been prescribed. "Give for 10 full days," "Continue for two weeks," "Give until finished," are not suggestions, but directions with a purpose. They should be considered orders.

INFANTS AND TODDLERS

Liquid medicines can be given to young children directly from a spoon (after careful measuring) or with a medicine dropper used to squirt the liquid slowly into a cheek. Take care to avoid directing the stream forcefully against the back of the throat and down the windpipe. Disguising medicine in a small quantity of juice, ice cream, applesauce, and the like is acceptable, provided the child takes the entire potion. A sweet treat may be offered after medication to cut the objectionable taste.

Although some infants and toddlers accept chewable tablets of medicine or even swallow whole tablets or capsules, these forms of medication are dangerous in this age group. A child under three can easily choke to death on a bulky pill. If liquid forms of the medicine are not available, tablets should be mashed and the contents of capsules emptied into juice or food before administering them to a toddler. Check with your doctor or pharmacist first—some medications should not be crushed or emptied.

OLDER CHILDREN

Many children over five or six can swallow tablets and capsules whole. Help your child to learn to swallow a pill by placing it on the back of his tongue before giving him something to drink, or include it in a half-teaspoonful of applesauce, jelly, or ice cream and have him swallow the entire thing. (A special glass that delivers a pill into the mouth automatically when the first gulp of the liquid in the glass is taken is also available.)

With the right approach you can easily get your child to take his medicine.

IMMUNIZATIONS

In the United States, it is generally recommended that children be immunized against eight potentially devastating diseases: diphtheria, tetanus, whooping cough (pertussis), polio, measles, mumps, rubella, and Hemophilus influenzae. Surveys repeatedly indicate that a large percentage of American children are inadequately protected against these illnesses, a result perhaps of a belief that some of these are extinct illnesses. However, as the percentage of children inoculated against a specific illness declines, the overall risk of that disease in a population increases, leading some experts to fear a resurgence of these deadly diseases. Discuss with your doctor any questions or fears you have about immunization. If your child has ever had convulsions or is ill at the time scheduled for an immunization, be sure to let your physician know beforehand.

DIPHTHERIA, TETANUS, AND WHOOPING COUGH (PERTUSSIS)

It is recommended that infants receive three injections of DTP (diphtheria, tetanus, pertussis) vaccine by age six months—starting at two months of age, and administered every other month. Following this initial series, they need a booster shot of DTP at age 18 to 24 months, and again at age four to six years. Thereafter, a booster shot of only diphtheria-tetanus vaccine is necessary every five to ten years for life.

Diphtheria. Cases of diphtheria are reported in every state every year. Before the general use of diphtheria toxoid, 80 percent of adults in this country were permanently immune to diphtheria because they had a clinical or subclinical form during childhood. This situation is no longer true. Consequently, adults should receive booster shots of diphtheria toxoid every 10 years. Serious reactions to diphtheria toxoid (a dead vaccine) are rare.

Tetanus. Cases of tetanus also occur every year. Although the toxoid vaccine is thoroughly safe and effective, its protection wanes over the years, and booster shots are required.

Whooping Cough. The whooping cough vaccine does not always result in complete immunity. Rare instances of permanent brain damage have followed its use. It is prone to cause brief reactions with fever. Boosters are not recommended routinely past the age of four to six years, when the dangers of whooping cough are judged less serious than the dangers of the vaccine. The mortality rate among infants with whooping cough under age one and the complication rate among older children are high enough to exceed by far the minimal risk of the vaccine.

POLIO

Infants should receive two or three doses of the live vaccine (Sabin, containing types 1, 2, and 3) orally, starting at two months with the second and third doses following, separated by one or two months. A booster series should be given at one and one-half to two years and at four to six years. Children not immunized during infancy should receive a total of three or four doses depending upon their age.

MEASLES, MUMPS, RUBELLA

The live, triple vaccine MMR should be given to all children at 15 months. It confers long-term and probably lifelong immunity against all three diseases.

Measles. Encephalitis occurs in one of every 1000 cases of natural measles. The risk of encephalitis from the vaccine is less than one in one million, and the disease complications of pneumonia and ear infections are never seen with immunization.

Rubella and Mumps. These diseases are relatively mild in children, but the first can be devastating to the unborn child, and the second can be complicated with encephalitis and orchitis. The vaccines are harmless to children (except for rare, transient arthritis in older children from rubella vaccine).

Prevention is the best medicine, and immunization is available for several deadly diseases.

CARING FOR YOUR CHILD

As a parent, you know better than anyone else when your child is not acting or feeling right. Sometimes there are visible signs of illness, like diarrhea or a fever; at other times, a change in your child's behavior alerts you to a problem, even though there are no physical symptoms. How can you better equip yourself to make the best decisions about your children's health?

First, educate yourself. Thoroughly read this book on childhood illnesses. Know what symptoms to watch for and what to do about them. Second, trust your instincts. If you feel there is a problem or an emergency situation, act on it. Third, ask questions. Don't be shy in dealing with doctors or other medical professionals; if you don't understand their answers, ask them to repeat the explanation.

Here are some rules of thumb about when to call the doctor for common ailments:

- Fever: higher than 101°F for more than 24 hours; the child looks and acts extremely ill, is difficult to rouse, or is incoherent.
- Common cold: lasts more than 10 days; accompanied by a fever higher than 101°F, a sore throat or pus-like nasal discharge for longer than two days, or a persistent cough or wheezing.
- Sore throat: pain present in throat for more than three days; accompanied by a fever higher than 101°F.
- Earache: pain lasts more than one hour; child looks very ill; child's temperature is higher than 101°F.
- Cough: accompanied by wheezing or difficulty in breathing; fever of more than 101°F; cough is persistent or is short, dry, and sharp; accompanying cold has lasted more than 10 days.
- Headache: frequent headaches; child appears ill.
- Stomach ache: pain is constant in the lower stomach for more than two hours; child has bloody stools; child vomits green or yellow matter more than twice.
- Vomiting: accompanied by fever; child is very ill—difficult to rouse; child vomits green or yellow matter more than twice; vomiting lasts more than 12 hours.
- Diarrhea: child does not urinate for eight hours; accompanied by vomiting; blood in the stools; diarrhea lasts more than one day; fever of more than 101°F.

Illness in babies may be a little harder to detect. Call the doctor when an infant:

- refuses to nurse or take liquids;
- urinates very little;
- vomits repeatedly;
- becomes extremely fretful or lethargic;
- becomes hoarse, has difficulty breathing, or has a crowing cry, especially if there is a fever and the baby appears sickly;
- becomes fretful and pulls on ear;
- has a marked increase in bowel movements; blood or mucus in the stool;
- displays noticeable protrusion of the soft spot on the head.

Call your doctor if an existing condition is not improving or if you do not know what to do about certain symptoms. Although parents need to use common sense in calling the doctor, it is always better to err on the side of being overcautious. A doctor can often give directions and reassure you over the telephone.

Respiratory disorders account for almost half of all childhood illnesses. Fortunately, they are easy to diagnose, and the availability of antibiotics makes many respiratory infections fairly simple to cure.

Although children are needy in the sense that they cannot provide for themselves, they are remarkably tough when it comes to recovering from illness and overcoming physical disorders. This resilience sees them through a time of life when their undeveloped bodies make them the most vulnerable to mishaps, accidents, and germs.

Animal Bites

DESCRIPTION

Animal bites that break the skin are cuts, puncture wounds, or scrapes and should be treated as such. But animal bites have other special characteristics: they are prone to infection because of bacteria in the animal's mouth, and they may cause lockjaw (tetanus) or rabies.

Rabies is a fatal disease of the central nervous system to which all mammals are susceptible. Transmitted through the saliva of the sick animal, rabies is most commonly found in the United States among skunks, foxes, cattle, dogs, bats, cats, and raccoons.

DIAGNOSIS

Bites are usually obvious from their appearance and from the child's telling of the tale. Claw wounds may be indistinguishable from bites but are treated in the same way because of contamination by the animal's saliva.

HOME TREATMENT

Wash the wound with soap and water and flush with water. Apply antiseptic to minor wounds. If a wild animal did the biting, catch and hold it if this can be done without endangering anyone else; otherwise, kill and preserve it for inspection of its brain for rabies. If it's a domestic animal, call the police to catch and impound it. Find out if the domestic animal was vaccinated against rabies and determine the child's tetanus toxoid status. Report the wound to your doctor immediately for advice concerning rabies, tetanus, and repair of the wound. In some states animal bites *must* be reported to the police.

PRECAUTIONS

● Keep children current on tetanus boosters. ● Always contact your doctor about treatment in the case of animal bites.

DOCTOR'S TREATMENT

Because of the high incidence of infection, your doctor may elect not to suture wounds. If cosmetic consideration necessitates closure, treatment first includes removal of the injured tissue and a thorough cleansing. Oral antibiotics may be prescribed. Also, your doctor will give a tetanus booster or human antitoxin to the patient if needed.

The decision whether or not to give antirabies vaccine, with or without antiserum, is complex. There's a good possibility of serious reactions. Your doctor will arrange for examination of the animal for the presence of rabies. A pet properly immunized against rabies can still transmit rabies, although this possibility is minimal. If the animal is not caught, the decision depends upon prevalence of rabies in your area, circumstances of the bite (provoked or unprovoked), and the species of the animal. Local health departments can provide information to help you make this decision. If you're still in doubt contact the Center for Disease Control, Rabies Investigations Unit, Atlanta, Georgia. Call for consultation, 8:00 a.m. to 5:00 p.m. E.S.T.—(404) 329-3311; off-duty hours, call (404) 329-2888.

Appendicitis

DESCRIPTION

Appendicitis is an infection (inflammation) of the appendix. The appendix is a hollow tube about the size of your little finger that forms a blind pouch at the site where the small intestine joins the large intestine. In 99 percent of all children the appendix lies in the lower right quarter of the child's abdomen. Appendicitis can occur at any age. If not surgically removed the infection worsens until the appendix bursts, and the infection spreads rapidly throughout the abdomen. An infected appendix may perforate (rupture) within hours of the initial pain, or not for a day or two.

DIAGNOSIS

Any abdominal pain in your child is due to appendicitis until proven otherwise. Typically, the pain of appendicitis is constant; it does not come and go as do cramps. Once it starts, it grows worse by the hour. The pain may start in the pit of the stomach, but it soon moves to the right, lower quarter of the abdomen. The pain is made worse by walking or just moving about. The abdomen is tender to a gentle pressure in the right, lower quadrant, more tender than in other areas. There may be nausea and vomiting, but these symptoms usually start only after the pain has started.

Generally, there is a low-grade fever (100°F, oral; 101°F, rectal), but the temperature may range anywhere from normal to 104°F. Bowel movements are usually normal, but there may be diarrhea. Urination may be painful. Diagnosis is difficult because all of these signs may not be present.

HOME TREATMENT

Try applying gentle heat, as with a heating pad turned to "low." If pain gets worse it is probably appendicitis. **Never apply cold;** this can mask symptoms of appendicitis. Aspirin and acetaminophen are safe but useless. Allow only clear liquids by mouth. **Never give a laxative or enema.**

PRECAUTIONS

• If pain persists in the lower, right quadrant of the abdomen for more than two hours despite home treatment measures, call your doctor.

DOCTOR'S TREATMENT

Because the only acceptable treatment for appendicitis is surgical removal of the appendix (an appendectomy), your doctor must be reasonably sure of the diagnosis. In addition to the abdomen, your child's chest and throat will be examined because a throat infection and pneumonia can mimic symptoms of appendicitis. A rectal examination will also be performed and a blood count and a urinalysis done. (These last two tests do not prove or disprove appendicitis, however.) An X ray may be called for.

Once tests are complete, your doctor may decide to operate or to admit your child to a hospital to watch him for a few hours until the diagnosis becomes more certain. Unjustified surgery is to be avoided, but the rule of safety is to operate on a child who may have appendicitis rather than postpone surgery until the appendix ruptures.

Asthma

DESCRIPTION

Asthma is an allergic reaction of the bronchial tree. It is a major and potentially dangerous form of allergy characterized by spasms of the smooth muscles of the bronchial tubes and the accumulation of thick mucus within these tubes. Shortness of breath, cough, sensations of air hunger, and wheezing are symptomatic, and it becomes harder for the child to breathe out than to breathe in. Wheezing is a high-pitched whistling sound more prominent on exhalation than on inhalation (in contrast to croup).

Asthma is caused by an allergy to inhalants (animal dander, pollens, dust, feathers, molds), and less commonly to foods, medicines, and insect stings. Attacks may be triggered by physical exertion, upper respiratory infections, emotions, or irritants such as smoke or chlorine. Fever is absent unless it is caused by a concurrent infection. The tendency to have allergies (including asthma) runs in families.

DIAGNOSIS

The characteristic sound of wheezing is an asthma "giveaway." The disease can be confirmed by rapid response to antiallergic medications. Asthma in a child under two is difficult to diagnose. History may be helpful, especially if an asthma attack either coincides with exposure to a cat, dog, horse, or other animal with hair or fur; is seasonal, as during tree, grass, or ragweed pollination; or occurs at night when the child is sleeping on a feather pillow.

HOME TREATMENT

No home treatment is recommended for the first attack; your doctor will confirm diagnosis and select a specific treatment. In an emergency, antihistamines may be given by mouth (in proper dose for weight) to allay the attack, but the treatment isn't reliably effective.

After the diagnosis is established, home treatment is important and effective. Prescribed medications should be administered promptly at onset of an attack; they are less effective after attack is under way. Rid your home of the identified causes of asthma allergy—pets, feather pillows and comforters, house dust, and sources of mold. Avoid exposing your child to such airborn irritants as insecticides, smoke, and paint fumes.

PRECAUTIONS

● Do not let an attack go untreated. Improperly treated, frequent attacks of asthma can result in permanent damage to the lungs and bronchial tubes.
● Because not all wheezes are asthma, have your doctor check your suspicions.

DOCTOR'S TREATMENT

Your doctor will initiate treatment by taking a complete and detailed history, conducting a physical examination (perhaps including an X ray) and running a series of five to twenty skin tests of suspected materials to which the child may be allergic. The substances identified as causes must be eliminated from the child's environment wherever possible. Diagnosis can be confirmed by response to medication.

Oral medications for use during an attack may include theophylline, aminophylline, ephedrine, metaproterenol, potassium iodide, antihistamines, and steroids. The same drugs may be recommended for daily use to prevent attacks. The newest medicines that can be used daily for prevention are cromolyn sodium and beclomethasone by inhalation. Children also may be desensitized to causative substances by weekly to monthly injections of increasing amounts of the irritating substances over a period of one to ten years. Severe attacks may require hospitalization for intravenous medications and fluids and for oxygen.

The treatment for asthma should produce good results. If the attacks do not lessen within one to three months, discuss a new approach with your doctor or ask for a second opinion.

Not all wheezes are caused by asthma. Check with your doctor.

Athlete's Foot

DESCRIPTION
Athlete's foot is an infection of the skin of the feet by one of several fungi that grow best in the presence of moisture. The mildest cases cause itching, scaling, and cracking between the toes, particularly between the fourth and fifth toes. Athlete's foot may spread to the soles of the feet as small blisters and scaling, and in severe cases may spread to the ankle and leg. It may invade and deform the toenails. Secondary infections caused by scratching may occur. The disease is commonest during adolescence, but it occasionally appears in infants.

DIAGNOSIS
Tentative diagnosis is based on the scaling and cracking appearance of the feet and the itching that accompanies it.

HOME TREATMENT
Apply fungicidal ointment once or twice a day (half strength for delicate skin), or use OTC ointments containing undecylenic acid, tolnaftate, or undecylenate. **Caution:** Many "incurable" cases of athlete's foot are not athlete's foot but are rashes from contact dermatitis caused by the treatment. Rubber-soled or plastic-soled shoes should be avoided for routine use to minimize sweating. Use cotton socks for absorption, preferably white to avoid contact dermatitis from dyes.

PRECAUTIONS
• Continue treatment until skin is completely clear; fungi not completely treated flare up. • If improvement is not prompt and lasting, see your doctor; your diagnosis may be wrong. • Many OTC medications for athlete's foot can cause contact dermatitis in susceptible people.

DOCTOR'S TREATMENT
Diagnosis is confirmed by scraping the skin and culturing the fungus or identifying it under a microscope. Your doctor may prescribe other fungicidal ointments or lotions or an oral fungicide. If a secondary infection is present, your doctor may prescribe oral antibiotics and soaking in a solution of potassium permanganate or aluminum sulfate and calcium acetate.

Use fungicidal ointment at the first sign of athlete's foot.

Bedwetting

DESCRIPTION

Many children cannot remain dry through the night before they are four or five. About ten percent of all children over the age of five are bedwetters. Children of any age may have occasional accidents at night, especially if ill or in exhausted sleep—conditions that do not represent true bedwetting (enuresis). Five to ten percent of children who bedwet have a physical disease such as an infection or abnormality of the urinary tract, diabetes, or neurological disorder. If a child wets himself both day and night, a physical disease is likely. Disease is also probable if enuresis develops a year or more after night training has been established. All other cases are considered functional; that is, no identifiable organ disorder is indicated as its cause. Some cases seem to be hereditary, with siblings and parents also having been bedwetters. Some are caused by overemphasis by the family on toilet training, others by taking children out of their night diapers too soon or by waking children to urinate in an effort to night-train. Some children have emotional problems that manifest themselves in bedwetting. Still, the cause of many cases of bedwetting remains unknown.

DIAGNOSIS

A child who consistently wets the bed after age five has enuresis.

HOME TREATMENT

Before any home treatment of chronic bedwetting can proceed, a complete urinalysis and urine culture should be done to rule out urinary tract infection and diabetes. Then, the best treatment is avoidance. **Do not** take a child out of night diapers until he consistently remains dry. **Do not** make a big fuss about daytime training. **Do not** try to shame a child into remaining dry at night. Withholding liquids during late afternoon and evening hours may be construed as cruel and undeserved punishment. Behavior modification techniques, with reward for success and neutral reaction toward failure, rarely work. Devices called enuratones, which awaken the child as urination starts, have been successful with older children but are not universally approved of by psychiatrists. Rubber sheets, draw sheets, and soakers are helpful until enuresis is corrected.

PRECAUTIONS

● Do not let a minor problem like enuresis become a major destructive factor in your relationship with your child. Anger and hate between parent and child are more costly than an extra wash. ● Do not allow siblings to taunt a bedwetter.

DOCTOR'S TREATMENT

Your doctor will insist first upon conducting a physical examination and urinalysis. The doctor may suggest X rays of the urinary tract or consultation with a urologist; imipramine (an antidepressant) by mouth at bedtime for a trial period; dextroamphetamine, dilantin, or caffeine, also on a temporary basis; or a program of behavior modification. All may be worth a try. There has been reported success with a special external catheter into which the penis is inserted at night.

Blisters

DESCRIPTION

Blisters are an accumulation of clear or almost clear fluid between layers of the skin. They may be caused by heat or chemical burns; rubbing (friction); infection by bacteria; viruses; hand, foot, and mouth disease; fungi; allergy to insect bites; or allergy to certain plants. Blisters range from the size of a pinhead to several inches.

DIAGNOSIS

The cause of blisters is determined by taking a history and noting location and appearance. When blisters appear on the palms or heels, they are usually due to friction (most blisters of the feet are caused by ill-fitting shoes and by not wearing socks); on the soles and toes they may be caused by a fungus; blisters on cuticles of fingers or backs of fingers almost always represent infection.

HOME TREATMENT

Do not break open blisters caused by friction or burns. Protect them with gauze and bandages. If accidentally opened, trim away the major portion of loose skin, cleanse with soap and water, and bandage. If the blister becomes infected (redness and increasing tenderness are signs of infection) it should be opened and soaked in an Epsom salt or Burow's solution (available over the counter).

PRECAUTIONS

● Red streaks spreading from a blister indicate spreading infection. ● Soaking unbroken blisters in too weak a solution causes marked enlargement of the blisters (suggested Epsom salts solution is at least four ounces salts to a quart of water).

DOCTOR'S TREATMENT

Your doctor will confirm your diagnosis and evaluate the presence and severity of infection. Infected blisters are opened and the fluid is cultured for type. Soaks or oral antibiotics may be prescribed individually or in combination.

Boils

DESCRIPTION

Boils are localized infections that occur beneath the skin. With rare exception, they are caused by a bacterium called hemolytic staphylococcus aureus—"staph" for short. They are characterized by redness, pain, and the formation of pus in the center, which tends to "point" (come to a head) and drain through the skin. Pus is a mixture of live and dead white blood cells, liquified dead tissue, and live and dead staph germs. Pus is therefore infectious and can spread boils to other areas and to other persons.

A small superficial boil is a *pimple* or *pustule*. (An acne pimple is not a true boil.) A large boil with multiple heads is a *carbuncle*. A boil on the edge of the eyelid is a *stye*. When many boils are present at one time the condition is called *furunculosis*. *Abcesses* are collections of pus in parts other than the skin, as in muscles, brain, bone, and internal organs. They are equivalent to boils but are often caused by germs other than staph.

Staph germs are often harmlessly present in the nose and throat and on the skin of well persons. They require a break in the skin to invade.

DIAGNOSIS

Diagnosis is determined by the presence of the above symptoms.

HOME TREATMENT

Boils respond to frequent or constant soaks with warm Epsom salts solutions (one-half cup per quart of water). When a boil comes to a head and drains, the drainage must be caught on a sterile bandage, and the surrounding skin sould be cleansed frequently with soap and water to avoid secondary boils. Boils that have come to a head but have not opened may be opened carefully with a sterilized needle, if your doctor agrees. Then the area should be soaked until pus, tenderness, and redness are gone.

PRECAUTIONS

● Be careful with boils on the face and forehead, including the nose and lips. The lymph and blood vessel drainage from these areas is partly internal. See your doctor. ● Never squeeze a boil. Squeezing disrupts the localizing wall formed by the body and may result in rapid spread of infection. ● Treat all minor wounds and insect bites properly to minimize the likelihood of boil formation.

DOCTOR'S TREATMENT

Your doctor may incise and drain the boil, culture the pus, and order sensitivity studies on the staph recovered to identify the antibiotic that will effectively fight the infection. Oral antibiotics will often be given. Many staph infections have become resistant to penicillin. Alternative antibiotics include erythromycin, oxacillin, cloxacillin, methicillin, and cephalosporin.

For chronic recurrent attacks of boils, your doctor may recommend nose and throat cultures of the patient and the entire family to identify carriers. Intranasal antibiotic ointments and antiseptic baths may be prescribed. Your doctor may suggest immunization against staph by regular injections of dead staph vaccine for extended periods (months or years).

Bronchitis

DESCRIPTION

Bronchitis is characterized by a dry, hacking cough; a low-grade (100°F, oral; 101°F, rectal) or no fever; and tightness and pain in the front, center of the chest. Loss of appetite and a general feeling of malaise are common. Cold symptoms may also be present. After a few days the cough loosens. Occasionally, a rattling sound can be heard in the chest when the child takes a breath, but there is never any real difficulty in breathing. The entire course of the condition may last more than a week.

Most cases are caused by one of many viruses. Bronchitis is contagious and is passed on in the same manner as a cold. If the disease recurs frequently, it may indicate that the child has an underlying allergy. (Sometimes children with asthma are unusually susceptible to recurrent attacks of bronchitis.)

DIAGNOSIS

Diagnosis is determined by the presence or absence of the above symptoms. There is rarely high fever or prostration, and the child experiences little or no breathing difficulty besides that caused by nasal obstruction. There is never pain on the side of the chest. No blood is present in the sputum.

HOME TREATMENT

Bronchitis is treated similarly to the way you would treat a common cold. Limited activity is recommended during the fever stage and the worst of the cough. Give aspirin or acetaminophen for fever and malaise (consult your doctor first). Nose drops may be used. A humidifier or vaporizer aids breathing. Cough medicine at bedtime or for an exhausting cough can be helpful. Encourage your child to drink liquids.

PRECAUTIONS

● See your doctor if any unusual symptoms occur such as pain on the side of the chest or blood in the sputum. ● See your doctor if bronchitis recurs more than once a year. ● See your doctor if the condition worsens instead of improving after three to four days. ● Avoid the use of oral decongestants, which may tighten the chest and aggravate a dry cough.

DOCTOR'S TREATMENT

Your child's physical examination should include a careful examination of his chest. Throat or sputum cultures, a chest X ray, and a blood count may be taken. If bronchitis is recurrent, your doctor will investigate allergy possibilities, the chance of a foreign body being in the bronchial tubes, or the presence of diminished immune mechanisms. The use of antibiotics and some types of cough medicines is debatable. Antibiotics often are not beneficial for most types of bronchitis, and some cough medicines can aggravate more than alleviate the condition.

Bruises

DESCRIPTION

Bruises consist of blood that has escaped from capillaries or larger blood vessels and is visible through the skin. They vary from pinhead-size to several inches in diameter, and usually are black and blue in color; if they are near the skin's surface they appear maroon or purple. Bruises of the whites of the eyeballs are always blood-red. As blood is reabsorbed, bruises often become yellow or green.

Most bruises are caused by physical trauma. Most normally active children always seem to have one or more bruises. Bruises take days or weeks to disappear, depending upon their size.

Bruises that appear spontaneously are cause for concern. These often appear in areas and in numbers that defy the likelihood that the cause has gone unnoticed. Spontaneous bruises result from abnormally fragile capillaries (as from scurvy or vitamin C deficiency), from capillaries injured by infections or allergic reactions, or from a deficiency of the clotting mechanisms of the blood.

There is one type of bruise known as a *petechia.* Petechiae are pinhead to one-eighth inch in size, are dark red or maroon in color, and are often present by the hundreds. Petechiae may appear from the neck up from forceful vomiting or coughing or in a localized area when caused by a blow.

DIAGNOSIS

A bruise of any size does not blanch when pressed upon, as do all other red or purple marks or rashes of the skin.

HOME TREATMENT

Cold applications soon after the injury occurs decrease bleeding and minimize bruising. *Warm* applications 24 or more hours afterward hasten reabsorption of the bruise.

PRECAUTIONS

● Spontaneous bruising should always be evaluated by a doctor. ● Petechiae scattered over the body can indicate an **urgent situation.** If fever or prostration is present, a true emergency exists. Don't waste any time; see your doctor at once.

DOCTOR'S TREATMENT

For traumatic bruises, a doctor's treatment is the same as the home treatment. For spontaneous bruises, including generalized petechiae, your doctor will give a complete physical examination including blood count; platelet count; blood coagulation studies; nose, throat, and blood cultures; spinal tap; and bone marrow studies. The patient may be hospitalized for administration of intravenous fluids and oral steroids and for antibiotic therapy.

Burns

DESCRIPTION

Burns are injuries of the skin caused by excessive heat, acids and alkalis, or electricity. Depth, extent, and location of the burn are important. Superficial burns (*first-degree*) cause reddening of the skin and pain; they may blister after one to two days. (Sunburn is a good example of a first-degree burn.) *Second-degree* burns redden and blister immediately. *Third-degree* burns are deepest and involve the death of a full depth of skin. The skin blisters or appears scorched (blackened) or dead white. The actual depth of a burn, except mild first-degree and severe third-degree conditions, cannot be reliably determined until healing starts.

Skin is a vital organ. If more than 10 percent of the skin area has suffered second- or third-degree burns, a serious emergency exists. If an area larger than the size of a child's palm receives a second-degree burn or any size area suffers a third-degree burn, consult your doctor. Burns of the fingers, joints, and face are threatening because of danger of scarring and deformity.

DIAGNOSIS

Redness, blistering, or scorching of the skin constitutes a burn. The problem is in deciding the degree and extent of the burn. Burns with no blistering or charring can be assumed to be first-degree.

HOME TREATMENT

Immediately apply cold water compresses to the burn. If the burn is a first-degree type, continue applications until the pain abates or up to one-half hour. If the burn is serious, cover it with a clean, cold, wet cloth; keep your child warm; and see your doctor at once. Do not apply ointments or other treatments to burns that will need a doctor's care.

PRECAUTIONS

● Burns are the second leading cause of accidental death among children under age four and the third leading cause among older children. **Prevention is paramount.** ● Water over 115°F can scald. Homes with children should have aquastats turned low. (The temperature of boiling water is 212°F.) ● Keep matches and cigarette lighters out of your child's reach. ● Do not keep gasoline or other inflammables in the home. Keep under lock and key outside. ● Avoid inflammable garments. ● Keep child-proof plugs in electrical outlets. ● Serious electrical burns are common as a result of young children chewing live electrical wires and extension cords. ● Second- and third-degree burns require up-to-date tetanus boosters.

DOCTOR'S TREATMENT

Your doctor will usually hospitalize your child for third-degree burns, second-degree burns that cover more than 10 percent of the skin, and for second-degree burns of the face, fingers, or joints.

Hospital treatment involves proper dressings, close attention to the need for intravenous fluids, attention to kidney and stomach complications, and sometimes antibiotics and plastic surgery.

Chicken Pox

DESCRIPTION

Chicken pox is caused by a specific virus that is highly contagious. The disease is contracted through the air from a person in the same room. There are no carriers. No one is naturally immune, not even newborn babies, but one attack gives lifelong immunity unless the attack is extremely mild. The incubation period is 10 to 21 days. No immunization is available yet.

Chicken pox may start with the symptoms of a mild cold, but usually a rash is the first sign. The rash worsens for three to four days, then heals in three to four days. The child is contagious from 24 hours before the rash appears until all blisters of the rash have dried. Fever can be low or as high as 105°F; fever is the worst on the third or fourth day after rash appears.

DIAGNOSIS

Diagnosis is made from the typical appearance of the rash. At first, each new spot resembles an insect bite, but within hours develops a small, clear blister in the center that may be hard to see without good light. Most blisters break and are replaced by a brown scab. The rash is distributed randomly all over the skin, including the scalp, and on the mucous membranes of the mouth, genitalia, anus, and eyelids. It becomes quite itchy. It never appears in bunches or groups. New lesions continue to appear hour by hour for three to four days. No other rash has all these characteristics.

HOME TREATMENT

Bed rest is not required, but your child should be isolated from others. Cut his fingernails to minimize the scratching. To reduce the itching, bathe your child in a tepid water-with-cornstarch bath, and apply calamine lotion to the skin with a soft brush. Anesthetic ointment may be applied to sore poxes around the anus and genitalia. Give acetaminophen for fever or pain.

PRECAUTIONS

• Chicken pox is dangerous to young babies, to patients on steroids or other immunosuppressant drugs, and to those with immune mechanism deficiencies. Report any known exposures or the onset of chicken pox in such children to your doctor. • Even though a sibling may already have been exposed, prevent further exposure because severity of the illness increases with the length of exposure. • Although it has not been proven that aspirin causes or promotes Reye's syndrome, it is recommended that aspirin not be given to a child with chicken pox. • Encephalitis is a rare complication; if high fever, prostration, headache, vomiting, or convulsions occur, see your doctor. • The pox may become infected, showing an increasing redness, soreness, and formation of pus. The lymph glands of the neck, armpits, groin, and back of the skull swell with chicken pox, but if they become red and tender they may be secondarily infected; report this to your doctor. • DO NOT apply calamine with phenol. • When your child is bathed, pat him dry without breaking the blisters or disturbing the scabs to avoid scarring. • If spontaneous bruising or ruptured blood vessels under the skin appear, see your doctor.

DOCTOR'S TREATMENT

Your doctor will usually culture an infected pox and will treat your child with oral antibiotics for five to ten days. (Antibiotics do not influence the *course* of the chicken pox, however.) If there are signs of encephalitis, your child will probably be hospitalized for tests and treatment. Spontaneous bleeding under the skin may be treated with oral medications, or your doctor may request hospitalization.

After a bath, pat your child dry to avoid breaking blisters.

Choking

DESCRIPTION

Choking is one of the few true emergencies of childhood in which minutes may determine life or death. There are only two causes: croup, especially bacterial; and foreign substances obstructing the airway.

Choking must be distinguished from gagging, which is much more common but not nearly as serious. Gagging is caused by a tickling or irritation of the throat or as a prelude to vomiting. There is only momentary interference with breathing, speaking, or crying. Choking is caused by the inability to take a breath, and is readily identified by the child's sustained, frantic efforts to breathe and by his inability to cry out or speak.

Breath-holding and a temporary stoppage of breathing during a convulsion may resemble choking; but in breath-holding there is no effort made to breathe. At the onset of a convulsion the child often cries out; there is no effort to breathe at first, and then breathing, though erratic, returns.

If choking continues, the child quickly becomes blue, convulsive, limp, and unconscious. **If the obstruction is complete you have between five and ten minutes to reestablish an airway before death occurs.**

The objects that choke children are usually of a shape and size to plug the opening of the larynx like a cork. Notorious items are peanuts, tablets, glass eyes of toy animals, hard or hard-coated candies, hot dogs, beads, popcorn, and tiny toys or small parts from toys. Solid particles of food from the stomach may choke a child who breathes during vomiting. A baby who vomits is safest from choking if he is lying on his stomach. A child may choke temporarily on liquids that "go down the wrong tube," but spontaneous coughing and deep breaths quickly relieve the problem.

DIAGNOSIS

The diagnosis depends on identifying the situation correctly according to the above description. There is frantic, unsuccessful effort to breathe. The child is silent.

HOME TREATMENT

Seconds count! Scream for help. A second adult on the scene should phone the police or paramedic squad for help. (Police are usually more quickly available in most communities than an ambulance, the fire department, or a doctor.)

First, give your child one minute to clear the obstruction by his or her own efforts. If this doesn't work, place your child head down over a chair, table, or your lap and pound hard on his back four times. Broken ribs heal, death does not. A baby may be held upside down by the ankles, but **always** support head and neck before pounding to avoid fracturing the neck.

If this is unsuccessful try the maneuver shown in the art on page 34. While standing to the child's back, press or squeeze vigorously and sharply on lower rib margins below the breastbone. You are trying to compress the upper abdomen and lower chest and to force the diaphragm up swiftly so that air in the lungs will pop the object causing the obstruction from the airway. Only if these safer measures fail should you consider reaching into the child's throat with a hooked finger in an effort to remove or dislodge the foreign body: there's a good chance of driving the object more tightly into the windpipe in your desperation to remove it. If your child is not breathing after the object is removed, give mouth-to-mouth resuscitation until trained help arrives.

PRECAUTIONS
● See precautions for choking due to croup. ● Never give mouth-to-mouth resuscitation until the obstructing object is removed; to do so may force the object further down the throat. ● Prevention of choking by foresight is most important: Examine all toys for loose eyes or other parts. Keep tablets under lock and key. ● Peanuts, popcorn, or hard candies should not be given to toddlers. (Clean up after adult parties before children can wander unattended into a room.) ● Plastic bags and balloons must be kept out of reach of small children.

Four sharp blows on the back may clear the obstruction.

continued

DOCTOR'S TREATMENT

When the obstruction is complete, the child seldom reaches a doctor in time. The obstruction may be incomplete even though you may not think so. Your doctor will operate, on the spot, to open the windpipe through the neck (tracheostomy). Then oxygen, artificial respiration, intravenous fluids, and blood tests will be administered.

Squeezing sharply and vigorously below the breastbone may force the object out of the air passage.

Colic

DESCRIPTION

The word *colic* means any cramp-like, intermittent abdominal pain. There are a variety of causes for all age groups. Infantile colic, or "three-month colic," is a specific problem that bothers ten to twenty percent of American babies. This form of colic starts during the first few weeks of life and lasts one to six months, (an average of three months). It takes the form of severe cramps of the digestive tract. An affected baby cries inconsolably for hours a day, particularly in the late afternoon and evening. He pulls his legs up, clenches his fists, screams, and turns red. He may nurse briefly but stops to return to crying. Rocking and cuddling interrupt the cries only briefly. In other respects the infant is normal; he gains weight well, has normal bowel movements, and doesn't spit up any more than most.

A variation of this classical form of colic is the infant past two weeks of age who wakes frequently (every two hours or so) cries fretfully, takes one to two ounces of formula or a few minutes at the mother's breast, falls into a fitful sleep, and wakens to repeat the sequence.

DIAGNOSIS

Diagnosis depends upon investigating and ruling out other probable causes. Although it's virtually impossible to pinpoint the cause of crying in babies this young, if the symptoms are evident and the treatment for colic brings relief, the condition is colic.

HOME TREATMENT

Check for obvious causes of discomfort other than colic: diarrhea or constipation; loose diaper pins; severe diaper rash; trapped arm or leg; whether baby is too hot or too cold; or signs of illness—fever, nasal discharge, cough, inflamed eyes, vomiting, hernia (lump in groin), or sores on the body. See whether your baby responds promptly to talking and cuddling and remains comfortable. (A baby in pain can be distracted, but only temporarily.) If breast-feeding, check that your nipples are not bleeding. Swallowed blood causes cramps. Offer your baby a bottle even if he has been fed recently and even if breast-fed. If your baby drinks generously and falls asleep comfortably for several hours, he was hungry, not colicky. Keep the baby partially upright in an infant carrier between feedings to rule out regurgitation of food into the esophagus.

PRECAUTIONS

● Make sure the formula is properly prepared. ● When bottle feeding your baby, be sure that the nipple is kept full to protect your baby from swallowing excessive air. ● Make sure that nipple holes are large enough that the baby will be satisfied in a reasonable time (less than 20 to 25 minutes). ● Burp the baby carefully in different positions after each feeding.

continued

DOCTOR'S TREATMENT

Your doctor will check for signs of illness—sores in the mouth, and urinary tract problems, for example. (A urinalysis may be ordered.) Your doctor also may recommend a change in formula to investigate the possibility of formula intolerance and will temporarily stop any solids already started to rule out food intolerance. An anticolic medicine will be tried for one to three days. Stomach relaxants may be given at each feeding or only at feedings near the times that the attacks of colic usually occur. In proper dosage, these medications will usually stop the discomfort of colic promptly (within one or two days). Generally, they will not stop pain from other causes, thus confirming the diagnosis of colic and treating it at the same time.

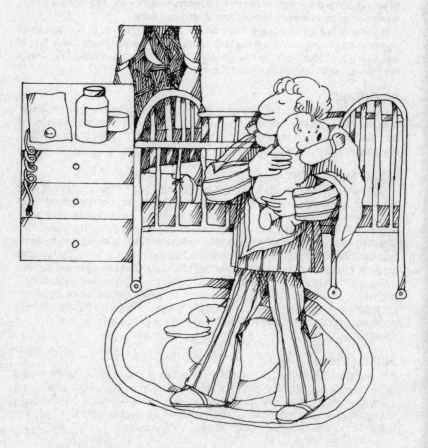

Cuddling provides only temporary relief from colic.

Common Cold

DESCRIPTION

A cold is a viral infection of the upper respiratory tract. It usually involves discomfort of the throat, nose, and paranasal sinuses, and sometimes the eyes (connected to the nose by the tear ducts), the ears (connected to the nose by the eustachian tubes), and the lymph nodes of the neck (connected by lymphatic channels). A cold is transmitted from person to person through the air, or via droplets on the hands and on inanimate objects (toys, drinking glasses, handkerchiefs). The incubation period is two to seven days. People of all ages are susceptible, but younger children and infants are particularly at risk.

Symptoms of a cold are nasal congestion, sneezing, clear nasal discharge, scratchy-sore throat, and fever up to 103°F. (In general, the younger the child, the higher the fever.) Symptoms may also include reddened, watery eyes; dry cough; mild swelling and tenderness of cervical lymph nodes; stuffiness; and mild pain in the ears.

Many fruitless years had been spent attempting to develop a vaccine against the cold germ before it was discovered that the germ is actually many different viruses, and all respiratory viruses can cause common colds. An attack by any of the more than 185 viruses confers immunity against only that virus and often only for a short time.

Many "cold viruses" can cause such complications as croup, laryngitis, bronchitis, viral pneumonia, and encephalitis. All cold viruses can render the child susceptible to secondary bacterial complications—ear infections, sinusitis, lymphadenitis, bacterial pneumonia. So no child's cold should be taken lightly.

DIAGNOSIS

It is impossible to diagnose a common cold with certainty. Confirming viral cultures and antibody studies is possible, but the cost is prohibitive. The diagnosis is usually guessed from the familiar symptoms, the absence of findings of other diseases, and by the fact that the ailment lasts only three to ten days.

HOME TREATMENT

Give acetaminophen for fever or pain. Use nose drops or oral decongestants and a nasal aspirator to relieve nasal stuffiness and discharge. Use cough medicines for easing a cough. Increase room humidity with a vaporizer or humidifier. Have your child drink a lot of liquids. Isolate him from others, particularly infant siblings and the elderly. Bed rest is not required, but do not allow strenuous physical activities while fever is present. Chest rubs and vitamin C treatments have not proven beneficial. Your child should eat only what he is able to.

PRECAUTIONS

• The following symptoms are usually absent from a common cold: fever lasting more than two to three days; pus-like discharge from eyes, nose,

continued

ears; large, red, tender neck glands; breathing difficulties; chest pain; severe headache; stiff neck; vomiting; shaking chills; and prostration. ● Some viruses that cause common colds are present in the body for one to two weeks, so the child remains contagious for the entire course of the cold. ● An infant is not protected against the common cold by the mother's antibodies and can become seriously ill from these viruses. Infants should not be exposed to siblings or others with "a mild cold."

DOCTOR'S TREATMENT

Your doctor can confirm the absence of other illnesses and complications by physical examination and sometimes will order a blood count and throat cultures. Otherwise, the course of therapy is the same as home treatment.

Treat the common cold with a humidifier and plenty of fluids.

Concussion

DESCRIPTION

A concussion is an injury to the brain from a fall or blow on the head by a blunt object. In many ways a concussion is like a bruise of the brain, with swelling and sometimes escape of blood into the brain tissue. Concussions may be mild to serious.

Most children sustain one or more blows to the head during childhood. Typical reactions are immediate crying, headache, paleness, vomiting once or twice, a lump or cut at the site of injury, and sleepiness for one or two hours. These are NOT the signs of a concussion.

Signs of possible concussion are any of the following: unconsciousness at instant of injury; no memory of accident or events preceding accident; confusion (child doesn't recognize parents or know his own name); persistent vomiting; inability to walk; eyes not parallel; pupils of different sizes (Note: some children have unequal pupils normally); failure of pupils to constrict when a bright light is shone into eyes; blood coming from ear canal; bloody fluid that does not clot coming from nose; headache that continues to increase in severity; stiff neck (chin cannot be touched to chest with mouth closed); increasing drowsiness; slow pulse (less that 50 to 60 beats per minute); and abnormal breathing.

There are two rare forms of concussion in which symptoms do not develop until hours after the injury (epidural bleeding) or until days or weeks afterward (subdural bleeding).

DIAGNOSIS

Diagnosis is made by looking for any of the symptoms listed above.

HOME TREATMENT

Essentially, treatment of a nonpenetrating head injury is either bed rest until the child has recovered, or surgery. Home treatment consists of keeping your child quiet, with his head on a pillow, and checking him frequently. He should be encouraged to sleep, but MUST be wakened every hour for evaluation of his condition until he feels well. Activity should be curtailed for at least one day after he is fully recovered. Give acetaminophen for headache.

PRECAUTIONS

● Do not attempt home treatment if any of the above signs of concussion is present. ● Do not treat at home if scalp is depressed at the site of injury or if a gentle thumping of the skull produces the dull sound of a broken melon (these findings are rarely, if ever, present without other signs of concussion). ● Do not give any medication stronger than acetaminophen.

DOCTOR'S TREATMENT

Your doctor may or may not order X rays of the skull (it is the substance of the brain that matters, not whether the skull is fractured or not), but your child may be hospitalized for observation. A CAT (computerized axial tomography) scan gives three-dimensional X rays of the brain, and is most useful. Echoencephalogram, electroencephalogram, and spinal-tap tests are sometimes helpful. A consultation with a neurosurgeon may be necessary.

Conjunctivitis

DESCRIPTION

Conjunctivitis, or pinkeye, is an infection of the transparent membrane (conjunctiva) that covers the white of the eye (sclera) and lines the undersurface of the eyelids. Conjunctivitis causes redness of the entire white of the eye and the accumulation of yellow pus. The eyelids may swell and redden, and there is a burning sensation in the eye. Vision is always normal, and light rarely bothers the eye.

Conjunctivitis is highly contagious—by contact with discharge from eye, or via objects (e.g, face cloths, toys, handkerchiefs) that have touched the infected eye or that have been handled by the child with conjunctivitis. Conjunctivitis usually spreads quickly to the opposite eye.

Conjunctivitis may exist alone or as a complication of sore throat, tonsillitis, or sinusitis. The incubation period is one to three days.

DIAGNOSIS

Conjunctivitis must be distinguished from other causes of reddened eyes. Eye allergies cause itching and tearing but never pain or pus. Viruses cause pain and tearing but no pus. Foreign bodies cause pain, sensitivity to light, and tearing, but no pus; redness is usually confined to one part of the white of the eye. Glaucoma causes pain, enlargement of the pupil, tearing, and sensitivity to light, but no pus. Diagnosis of conjunctivitis is a process of eliminating these other possibilities.

HOME TREATMENT

Isolate your child. Frequently instill antibiotic eye drops or ointment into the eyes. A doctor's prescription is required, but often your doctor will oblige you by phone if your description is detailed and accurate. Treat both eyes even though only one seems involved. Continue treatment for 24 hours after the eyes appear normal. Watch other members of the family for symptoms.

PRECAUTIONS

● With medication, improvement should be prompt—within 24 hours. If eyes don't clear, call your doctor. ● If eye ointments are used, there will be blurring of vision for a few minutes after each application. Any other disturbance of vision should be promptly reported to your doctor. ● Be certain to notify your doctor of any other signs of illness, such as head cold, nasal discharge, sore throat, fever, or sore glands.

DOCTOR'S TREATMENT

Careful examination of the outside and inside of the eyeball, including looking under the eyelids for hidden foreign bodies, is part of the doctor's treatment. Your doctor may stain the eyeball with special drops to detect injuries or ulcers and culture the eye, nasal, and throat discharge. Oral antibiotics or consultation with an ophthalmologist may be necessary.

Constipation

DESCRIPTION

Constipation means that bowel movements (BMs) are too hard. Frequency is not a factor. Passage of six too-firm BMs a day is considered constipation. Passage of one BM every third or fourth day of normal or soft consistency is not constipation. Many normal, healthy children have a BM only every few days and are not constipated. The hardness of a stool is judged by appearance, by feeling, and by diameter. A stool greater than twice normal diameter must be too hard.

Constipation has either a physical, organic cause or a functional cause. Organic causes are rare and relatively easy to diagnose.

Over 95 percent of constipation cases are functional and involve no physical abnormality. Functional constipation can always be cured by diet changes and daily use of stool softeners. The function of the large bowel (colon) is to store unabsorbed food waste and to absorb and conserve water from the liquid material received from the small intestine. Factors that favor the absorption of too much water by the colon lead to constipation. In children there are two common factors. The first is that the diet does not include enough roughage, which retains water. Foods that prevent constipation are: all fruits except bananas—particularly those fruits eaten with their skins on—and fruit juices; all vegetables except peeled potatoes, especially if eaten raw; and unrefined grains. All other foods, including milk, promote constipation.

The second factor that leads to constipation is when the child resists the normal impulse to move the bowels and retains the stool. This practice permits the absorption of water by the intestine and results in stools that are too hard. The most common reason for a child's retention of the stools is his parents being overzealous in their efforts to toilet train. Passage of the too-hard stool causes pain, which reinforces the child's determination to postpone the next BM. Constipation overdistends the large bowel, causing a loss of muscle tone; and the impulse to empty the bowel becomes weaker. This cycle can lead to chronic constipation. Constipation can cause pain in the anus at defecation and can result in the presence of red blood on and around the BM. Other symptoms are cramps and loss of appetite.

DIAGNOSIS

Diagnosis is made by observing the character of the BM, including its diameter. However, if constipation has been present for days and weeks, paradoxical diarrhea may develop. In this condition loose, watery BMs seep around the hard stool in the colon and are passed as diarrhea. This can confuse the diagnosis.

HOME TREATMENT

For immediate, temporary relief, give an enema (disposable commerical enemas are the most convenient) or use a glycerine suppository. For a long-term permanent cure, increase the amount of roughage and decrease the amount of constipating foods in your child's diet. Since children often can-

continued

not be easily induced to eat what they should, it is often necessary to supplement their daily diet with artificial stool softeners. Stop efforts to potty train temporarily.

PRECAUTIONS
● Laxatives may force passage of a hard stool and cause pain that leads to further holding back by the child. ● Enemas, suppositories, and laxatives are habit-forming.

DOCTOR'S TREATMENT
Your doctor will confirm diagnosis of constipation if necessary by rectal examination and careful palpation of the child's abdomen. X-ray studies of the bowel may be required to rule out organic causes. Detailed directions and follow-up by your doctor may be necessary.

Foods that can prevent constipation are: fruits, raw vegetables, and unrefined grains.

Coughs

DESCRIPTION

Coughing is a valuable defense mechanism that guards the respiratory tree against foreign material. Not a disease itself, coughing is a reflex that is set off by any foreign matter that has entered or seeks to enter the respiratory tree and by any irritation of the lining of the tree. (The respiratory tree includes the throat, larynx, trachea, bronchial tubes, and lungs.) Most often, coughing is beneficial, but sometimes it is ineffective. The chief harm it can produce is interference with sleep and exhaustion from muscular effort. Coughing also may lead to vomiting; and in young infants, if severe and prolonged enough, may result in injury to the bronchial tree.

Most coughs are caused by viruses (common colds, croup, bronchitis). Some are caused by bacteria (sinusitis, epiglottitis, bacterial pneumonia, pertussis), some by allergies (asthma), and some by inhaled foreign bodies.

DIAGNOSIS

A cough is only as serious as the disease or condition that causes it. As with a fever, a child with a cough is no less ill if you suppress the cough. A child with a mild illness and a cough is still only mildly ill.

HOME TREATMENT

Cough medicines are intended to: reduce the frequency of the cough by suppressing the cough reflex; loosen a tight cough; dry up a loose cough; or combat an allergy responsible for coughing. They often contain ingredients to accomplish more than one of these goals at the same time. Before purchasing a cough medicine for home use, determine which of the four goals listed above you want accomplished and consult your pharmacist.

PRECAUTIONS

● Do not give cough medicine to a child with croup. ● Do not give cough medicines to a child who may have inhaled a foreign body.

DOCTOR'S TREATMENT

Your doctor will direct treatment toward the condition causing the cough, not at the cough itself. Narcotic cough medicines and some with antihistamines require a doctor's prescription.

Coughing is a protective reflex.

Cradle Cap

DESCRIPTION

Cradle cap (seborrheic dermatitis) consists of adherent yellowish, scaly or crusted patches on the scalp, composed largely of oil and dead cells. It is most common in infants but is seen in children through age five. The disease may extend onto the forehead and may also be present in the skin fold behind the ears, on the ears, and in the diaper area. The most typical location is over the anterior fontanel (the soft spot). Temporary loss of hair is common.

DIAGNOSIS

Diagnosis can be made from the locations and appearance of the patches and by the greasy scalp film that can be scraped off.

HOME TREATMENT

Mild cases of cradle cap on the scalp can be cured by daily, vigorous shampooing using soap on a wet, rough facecloth wrapped around the palm of your hand. Special shampoos that contain coal tar or salicylic acid are useful. Apply ointments containing sulfur, salicylic acid, or coal tar to the scalp and other areas daily.

PRECAUTIONS

● Be sure that medicated shampoos and ointments do not get into your child's eyes. ● Discontinue using these preparations if irritation and reddening of the scalp or skin occur.

DOCTOR'S TREATMENT

Your doctor will confirm diagnosis by differentiating cradle cap from eczema, yeast infections, and contact dermatitis. The doctor's treatment will be the same as home treatment. In addition a steroid cream or ointment may be prescribed.

Vigorous shampooing will cure cradle cap.

Crossed Eyes

DESCRIPTION

Infants learn to focus their eyes during their first three to six months. Occasionally, their eyes turn in or out in relation to each other. These conditions may briefly occur even up to age one and still be considered normal. When an infant's eyes are continuously not parallel, when they are not parallel with increasing frequency at any age, or when they are not parallel past age one, the situation is abnormal and requires your doctor's advice.

Most cases of crossed eyes result from improper functioning of the extraocular muscles. Some are caused by a visual defect in one or both eyes. Anything that can cause the eyes to cross can also cause the development of a "lazy eye." If this condition is not corrected by age seven, loss of sight due to disuse may result.

DIAGNOSIS

Diagnosis is made by observing the relationship of the eyes to each other as the child focuses near and far, and looks to either side and up and down.

Most crossed eyes reported by parents is an optical illusion, and the child's eyes are actually straight. Many infants and young children have an extra skinfold at the nasal side of the eyelids, present because of the tininess of the bridge of the nose. This extra fold allows more of the white of the eye to show toward the temples than toward the nose, creating an illusion of crossed eyes. Straightness of the eyes is best judged by observing the position of the reflected points of light in both eyes (highlights). Identical location of the highlights in both eyes proves eyes are parallel.

HOME TREATMENT

There is no home treatment except under supervision and instruction by your doctor.

PRECAUTIONS

● If the pupils of your child's eyes are not equally black, smoothly round, and the same size, report to your doctor. ● If your child's eyes are not parallel, see your doctor. ● Visual acuity (sharpness of vision) should be checked annually in all children from age three.

DOCTOR'S TREATMENT

Your doctor will check extraocular muscles and vision and inspect the inside of the eyeballs. This examination can be done on any child at any age. If diagnosis of crossed eyes is confirmed, treatment will depend upon the cause. It may include eye surgery, glasses, patching of one eye, daily use of eye drops, or eye muscle exercises guided by a specialist. Your doctor will probably recommend that you consult an ophthalmologist (a physician who specializes in eyes.)

Croup

DESCRIPTION

Croup is a common, contagious illness of children contracted in the same manner as a common cold—by airborne droplets and direct contact with an infected person. Croup is characterized by a tight, dry, barking cough and by hoarseness. Difficult breathing develops quickly with more pronounced trouble breathing *in* than breathing *out.* This is the opposite of that seen in asthma. Efforts to breathe in cause the typical crowing sound associated with croup.

Basically, there are three types of croup: diphtheria, spasmodic croup, and epiglottitis. *Spasmodic croup* is common and is usually caused by a virus. Spasmodic croup most often occurs between three months and three years of age and represents an infection of the vocal cords and voice box (larynx). It is similar to laryngitis in the adolescent or adult. Fever is absent or low-grade (101°F). The disease may occur once in a child, or repeatedly with every head cold. Children who experience recurrent croup often develop other forms of respiratory allergies later. Spasmodic croup can be serious, but milder cases, especially recurrent ones, can be safely handled at home.

Epiglottitis is a severe, rapidly progressive, **life-threatening illness**—a true emergency in which minutes count. It is an infection of the epiglottis (covering of the larynx) and adjacent tissues caused by bacteria. Epiglottitis croup has all the symptoms of spasmodic croup. It is most common in children between three and nine years of age. There is also a rising fever from 103°F to 105°F. Difficulty with breathing increases progressively and your child may have trouble swallowing, preferring to sit with his head forward, mouth open, and tongue partially out. The condition rapidly progresses to choking, convulsions, and death if untreated.

DIAGNOSIS

The combination of a barking cough, hoarseness, difficult breathing, and a crowing sound on inhalation is obvious croup. For all practical purposes, diphtheria can be ruled out as a cause if your child has been properly immunized. Choking on an aspirated foreign object may resemble croup but can also be ruled out by history, fever (if present), and the ability of the child to talk.

In epiglottitis croup a definitive diagnostic sign is the appearance of a swollen, red epiglottis at the base of the tongue. (Use a flashlight to look, but **do not depress the tongue** in an effort to see the epiglottis as this may cause instant and complete obstruction of the air passage.)

It is important to always consider the possibility of epiglottitis as a cause of croup when any of the above symptoms are present.

HOME TREATMENT

Use steam from a vaporizer or humidifier. Steam also may be generated quickly and temporarily by running a hot shower in a closed bathroom. Sit in the room with your child for a short while. In spasmodic croup, especially without fever, a single, large, oral dose of a steroid, given with your doctor's permission, can be miraculous, giving relief in 15 minutes. Unless you have witnessed croup before, it is best to consult your doctor with first attack.

PRECAUTIONS

● Never give suppressant cough medicines to a child with croup. ● If you suspect epiglottitis, notify your doctor and head for the nearest hospital emergency room.

DOCTOR'S TREATMENT

For spasmodic croup, your doctor's treatment will be the same as your home treatment. However, the doctor may hospitalize your child and use a croup tent with high humidity, order cultures and blood count, prescribe antibiotics, and use isoproterenol by inhalation. If the condition becomes severe, your doctor may have to perform a tracheostomy.

Epiglottitis is always treated as an emergency. Your child may be intubated (have a tube inserted in his airway). If necessary, a tracheostomy is performed, intravenous fluids and antibiotics are given, and the child is monitored.

Steam from a vaporizer is helpful in treating croup.

Cuts

DESCRIPTION

If a cut is more than skin deep, it cannot be treated at home. Deeper structures, such as muscles, tendons, nerves, and deeper layers of the scalp, must be repaired by sewing. A laceration with ragged edges or one that is deeply embedded with dirt needs professional care to avoid infection and to minimize scarring.

A cut heals leaving a scar the size of the opening of the skin. No treatment will reduce the length of a cut or resulting scar, but the closer the edges of the cut are to one another during the healing process, the narrower the final scar. If the edges of the cut can be held together by bandaging at home there may be no advantage to a doctor's treatment. However, if the cut involves an area that moves, such as that near a joint or parts of the face, it is virtually impossible to keep the edges from gaping without the wound being sewn. A small cut rarely requires suturing to control the bleeding.

DIAGNOSIS

Whether a cut needs a doctor's care depends upon careful inspection after the bleeding has stopped. You must evaluate the width and depth, the dirtiness and raggedness, and whether a home-style bandage can hold the edges together for the seven to ten days required for healing.

HOME TREATMENT

First, stop the bleeding by applying firm pressure directly on the cut for 10 minutes (by the clock). Use sterile gauze if it's immediately available, but any reasonably clean cloth—a handkerchief, towel, or shirt—will do. Even bleeding from large arteries can be controlled by direct pressure. Only if a limb is partially or completely amputated will a tourniquet be necessary.

Second, once the bleeding has stopped, wash the area with soap and water so that the cut is clearly visible. If home treatment appears reasonable, apply a nonstinging antiseptic and draw the wound's edges together with adhesive butterflies or Steristrips bandages (both available at your pharmacy). Cuts near the joints of your child's fingers can be immobilized by splinting the fingers till the cut has healed. Cuts between the toes can sometimes be immobilized by bandaging adjacent toes together. Cover the wound with sterile dressing, inspect it every day for infection, and remove butterflies or Steristrips bandages after seven to ten days.

PRECAUTIONS

● If the laceration requires sewing, it must be done within eight hours to avoid infection. ● If the home-treated wound becomes infected (showing increased tenderness, swelling, discharge of pus, or red streaks radiating from wound), see your doctor. ● Be sure that tetanus immunization is current.

DOCTOR'S TREATMENT

A doctor, surgeon, or plastic surgeon has facilities and skill to handle cuts that are beyond home care.

Deafness

DESCRIPTION

Normal hearing depends upon sound waves passing down the ear canal and setting the eardrum to vibrating; that, in turn, moves the three tiny bones in the middle ear. This motion is transmitted across the middle ear to the inner ear (cochlea), where the vibrations are changed to electrical impulses that are carried to the brain via the eighth cranial nerve and are interpreted as sound by the brain. Damage, disease, or malfunction of any of these structures can result in deafness.

A hearing loss may be slight or severe. It may involve one or both ears and may be present at birth or develop at any age.

DIAGNOSIS

Suspect hearing loss if any of the following symptoms are observed: your infant over three months old ignores sounds or does not turn head toward sound; your baby over one year old does not speak at least a few words; your child over two years old does not speak in at least two- to three-word sentences; your child over five years old does not speak so that a stranger can understand him; your child has learning problems in school at any age; or your child does not appear to hear well at home. Any of these symptoms may be caused by hearing loss, but they also may be the result of other causes.

HOME TREATMENT

Treatment depends upon the cause, as well as upon the degree of the hearing loss.

PRECAUTIONS

● If you are a woman of child-bearing age, consult your doctor about rubella immunization. A simple blood test will determine whether or not you've been immunized. ● Do not put any object, including cotton swabs, into your child's ear canal for any reason. You may impact the wax or damage the eardrum.

DOCTOR'S TREATMENT

Your doctor will examine the ear to determine the cause of deafness. Hearing can be tested by specialists in children of any age past early infancy by various devices and instruments. There are federally funded speech and hearing centers in all states to which a doctor can refer your child if diagnosis, cause, or treatment of hearing loss is in doubt. Your deaf child should start special education as soon as the condition is discovered, even if he is as young as one or two years old.

Dehydration

DESCRIPTION

Dehydration means drying out. It is caused by the loss of fluids from the body in excess of the amount of fluids taken in. In addition to the loss of water, dehydration is accompanied by the loss of minerals and salts from the body. Fluids, minerals, and salts are lost from the body through diarrhea, vomiting and sweating, through water vapor from the lungs with excessive breathing (as in asthma), and in the urine (in diabetes). The quantity of water in the body and the proper concentration of salts and minerals are vital to health and to life.

The smaller the child, the more quickly dehydration can develop. In young infants dehydration occurs as rapidly as 12 to 24 hours from onset of one of the above causes. Dehydration as a result of diminished intake of liquids in a child who is not losing fluids from some other cause is rare. Except in young infants and in children with diabetes, the kidneys can compensate for small fluid intake. But a diminished intake of liquids in a child who is also losing fluids hastens dehydration.

DIAGNOSIS

Except in the presence of diabetes, dehydration can be detected by observing the urinary output. A young child who goes six to eight hours without urinating and an older child who does not urinate for ten to twelve hours may be dehydrated. Other signs of dehydration include: sunken eyes; dryness (to an exploring finger) of the membranes of the mouth; loss of elasticity of the skin when pinched between the thumb and forefinger; drowsiness; rapid or slow breathing; and depression of the soft spot in an infant.

HOME TREATMENT

Vomiting, if present, must be stopped. With any condition that causes fluid loss—including prolonged high fever—you should encourage your child to drink extra fluids. The best liquids to give a child with a severe case of dehydration are commercial fluids that contain proper salts and sugar. Other good liquids are gelatin desserts (liquid or jelled), weak tea with sugar, ginger ale, colas and other carbonated drinks, and fruit juices. Plain water is less helpful. Whole milk and skimmed milk diluted by a half with water are sometimes tolerated.

PRECAUTIONS

● **Undiluted skimmed milk and boiled whole milk are forbidden** because the salt and mineral content is too great for the child to tolerate. ● If symptoms of dehydration develop, contact your doctor; the younger the child, the more urgent the situation. ● Urinary output is totally unreliable in judging dehydration in a diabetic.

DOCTOR'S TREATMENT

Your doctor will diagnose and treat the underlying condition. Your child may be admitted to a hospital for intravenous fluids and salts and for tests to detect salt and mineral disturbances.

Diaper Rash

DESCRIPTION

Rashes in the diaper area may be due to the chemicals used in washing cloth diapers—detergent, bleach, whitener, water-softener, or soap—or to the chemicals used in the manufacture of disposable diapers. Diaper rashes are red, slightly rough and scaly, and distributed over the total area touched by the diapers. A variant of diaper rash is caused by the plastic outer layer of the disposable diapers or by the plastic or rubber pants worn over cloth diapers. Other rashes in this area include:

Ammonia rash, in which the skin is burned by ammonia from urine decomposed by normal bacteria of the skin. This condition is worse after long sleep. It is identified by an ammonia smell when changing the diaper.

Yeast rash, which is common during the first weeks of life and after the child has been given antibiotics. The rash is composed of countless red, scaly spots, each several pinheads in size and representing a colony of yeast. The spots may all run together into a solid area, but identifiable islands are present at the edge of the rash. It is caused by the same fungus (monilia) that causes thrush. Lesions in the mouth help confirm identification of the rash.

Food and drug rashes, which occur in allergic children and are caused by new foods or medications. There is often a rash on the cheeks of the face present at the same time.

Infectious rashes, which are an infantile form of impetigo and are identified by blisters that contain pus. The blisters are generally match-head size and smaller than the impetigo that occurs in the older child.

Seborrhea, a common rash in the skin creases of the diaper area. It is usually accompanied by seborrhea elsewhere, such as on the scalp (cradle cap) and behind the ears.

Contagious disease rashes such as the rashes that accompany chicken pox, measles, and scarlet fever. Sometimes the rash appears in the diaper area a day before it spreads to more typical areas.

DIAGNOSIS

Diagnosis depends upon history—a recent change to different diapers or the manner of laundering them, new foods, or treatment with antibiotics—as well as appearance and location of rash, presence of ammonia odor, and the presence of lesions elsewhere on the body.

HOME TREATMENT

Change soap brands or the method of washing the diapers. Apply protective ointments (petroleum jelly, zinc oxide, vitamin A & D ointment, or Desitin ointment). For rash from ammonia use anti-ammoniacal powders and ointments. Avoid airtight outer covering over diapers. If rash is severe, your doctor can prescribe oral medications. For rash from foods and drugs eliminate new foods, beverages, and medicines started in the past month. (Check with your doctor first.) Apply steroid preparations locally. Then re-introduce stopped foods one at a time at weekly intervals in order to determine the

continued

offender. For rash from infections wash with soap and water and apply anti-biotic ointment (bacitracin, neomycin) frequently. If rash is spreading or severe, or if it is accompanied by fever, irritability, or loss of appetite, see your doctor.

PRECAUTIONS
● If the rash gets worse even after two days of home treatment, reassess your diagnosis or see your doctor. ● Do not use ointments in combination (those that contain an antibiotic, fungicide, and steroid) without your doctor's approval. ● If your child has any other symptoms see your doctor.

DOCTOR'S TREATMENT
Your doctor will identify a rash by appearance and history and may culture or scrape the rash for identification of bacteria or fungi. Oral antibiotics or medicated ointment may be prescribed for diagnostic/therapeutic trial.

Not every rash in the diaper area is necessarily diaper rash.

Diarrhea in Children

DESCRIPTION

Diarrhea refers to the looseness of the stools and not to the frequency of bowel movements (BMs). The number of BMs per day measures the severity of the diarrhea. The condition in children over the age of five differs in several respects from that which occurs in infants. The likelihood of dehydration decreases with the increasing age and size of the child. Serious dehydration is unlikely past six years old unless diarrhea is accompanied by vomiting that interferes with liquid intake. Intestinal viruses are the most common cause of diarrhea in older children, followed by dysentery bacteria and intestinal parasites. Respiratory viruses and food intolerances are the least likely cause of this condition in older children. Other causes of diarrhea, which are rare or unknown in infants but prevalent in older children and which can produce prolonged and recurrent illness, include ulcerative colitis and regional enteritis (Crohn's disease)—inflammatory diseases of unestablished cause.

DIAGNOSIS

As in infants, the diagnosis depends upon character of the stool and upon the child's history.

HOME TREATMENT

If present, treat vomiting first. Limit or eliminate solids, especially those with roughage; fruits (except bananas); vegetables; butter and fatty meats; and peanut butter. Eliminate milk since diarrhea often causes temporary intolerance to milk, which further aggravates diarrhea. Encourage clear liquids.

Kaolin and pectin mixtures (available OTC) may slow diarrhea, but do little for cramps. Consult your doctor about using prescription anti-diarrheal remedies.

PRECAUTIONS

● Isolate an infant from siblings who are ill with vomiting and diarrhea.
● Report blood in stools, high fever, prostration, severe or prolonged (more than two days) diarrhea to your doctor; dysentery may be the cause.
● Report frequently recurrent diarrhea to your doctor since the diarrhea may be a symptom of colitis or enteritis, especially if there is weight loss.

DOCTOR'S TREATMENT

Your doctor's treatment will be the same as home treatment. Blood tests, X rays of large and small bowels, sigmoidoscopy, intestinal antibiotics, and steroids also may be necessary. In severe cases, hospitalization may be ordered.

Diarrhea in Infants

DESCRIPTION

Diarrhea refers to the consistency of the stool and not to the frequency of bowel movements (BMs). Any BM that is partially or completely runny constitutes diarrhea. The loose and watery stools often contain mucus and sometimes flecks of red blood, and BMs number from one to twenty per day. (The frequency and volume of the loose stools is a measure of the severity of the diarrhea.) Diarrhea may be accompanied by cramps and sometimes fever, loss of appetite, vomiting, and weight loss. The condition in infants and young children is potentially dangerous because of the increased likelihood of dehydration.

The usual causes of diarrhea are infections of the digestive tract and intolerance to foods. In infants, infections may be caused by respiratory viruses as well as intestinal viruses, bacteria, and parasites. Two examples of foods that may be inherently improper for infants in general are corn kernels or large quantities of prunes. Other foods may be wrong for a particular infant with food intolerances or allergies. Many antibiotics also may cause diarrhea in infants.

DIAGNOSIS

The character of the stools is definitive. One or two loose BMs followed by a return to normal does not represent a significant case of diarrhea. The cause of diarrhea may be suggested by the foods recently added to the infant's diet, cases in older siblings, or recent antibiotic therapy.

HOME TREATMENT

If present, vomiting must be treated first. Eliminate all newly introduced foods and beverages. If diarrhea is mild, eliminate foods with roughage. Stop all fruits (except bananas) and vegetables, and minimize fruit juices. If diarrhea is mild, dilute milk by half with water; if diarrhea is severe, eliminate all solids and milk altogether. Encourage the child to drink liquids.

Check with your doctor about using anti-diarrhea medications.

PRECAUTIONS

● Continue treatment until there are normal stools. ● Solids aggravate diarrhea and can be avoided for several days without any danger to general health. Liquid intake is of paramount importance. ● Watch for symptoms of dehydration. ● Improperly prepared and refrigerated formulas are a common cause of serious infant diarrhea, especially under primitive conditions of sanitation (camping and traveling).

DOCTOR'S TREATMENT

Your doctor's procedure will be the same as your home treatment, but your doctor may want to evaluate the seriousness of dehydration. (The loss of 10 percent of a baby's weight indicates serious dehydration.) Stools may be cultured for bacteria. Hospitalization may be required for administration of intravenous fluids and for investigation of a possible malabsorption problem.

Diphtheria

DESCRIPTION

Diphtheria is a frequently fatal disease caused by a specific bacterium and caught by exposure to a person with the disease or to a carrier of the disease. The germ causes infection of the nose, throat, tonsils, and lymph nodes of the neck. The microorganism kills, sometimes by destroying tissue, and sometimes by producing a toxin that causes heart damage and paralysis. The incubation period is two to four days. The infected throat develops pus and a gray membrane that looks similar to strep throat and mononucleosis. Croup and pneumonia are common complications.

The protective immunization against diphtheria has been available for over 40 years and is among the safest, cheapest, and most effective of all known vaccines. Despite the availability of the vaccine, diphtheria still exists throughout the world.

DIAGNOSIS

Diphtheria is difficult to diagnose for three reasons: First, many American doctors have never seen a case in training or practice. Second, diphtheria closely resembles mononucleosis, strep throat, and other forms of croup. And finally, routine throat cultures taken in a doctor's office for detection of strep do not show diphtheria bacilli. (Twenty percent of diphtheria cases also have strep as a secondary infection in the throat.) Diagnosis is made by appropriate cultures of the nose and throat.

HOME TREATMENT

It is imperative that children be routinely immunized for diphtheria during infancy. Three shots are required the first six months of life. Routine boosters are required at 18 to 24 months and at age five. Boosters are further required every 10 years thereafter. There is no home treatment for diphtheria, but if your child has not been immunized, every cough, sore throat, or case of croup could be the onset of diphtheria.

PRECAUTIONS

● If your child is not up-to-date on immunization against diphtheria, be sure to inform the doctor treating your child. Diphtheria may be the furthest thought from your doctor's mind. ● Consider that an unimmunized child can contract diphtheria from a well child or from an adult who is a carrier. ● Never travel to an underdeveloped country where diphtheria is prevalent without immunization.

DOCTOR'S TREATMENT

If your doctor suspects diphtheria, he or she can diagnose and treat the disease. Diphtheria antitoxin, steroids, or large doses of penicillin or erythromycin are effective therapies if started early enough. A tracheostomy may be required if the condition is severe.

Dislocated Elbow

DESCRIPTION

A dislocated elbow is the only common dislocation in young children. Actually, a dislocated elbow is an incomplete dislocation, therefore more properly called a "subluxation." Also known as "nursemaid's elbow," it frequently occurs between one and three years of age and is rare beyond four.

Dislocation usually occurs when there is a sudden yank on the child's hand or wrist as the parent attempts to save the child from a stumble or fall. It may also be the result of a child being swung around by the wrists in a game or by his grabbing a handhold to prevent falling.

Once the accident occurs, immediate pain results and is located anywhere from the elbow to the wrist. The child refuses to use the affected arm, clutching it to his side with the good arm. Swelling of the wrist and hand develops several hours later.

DIAGNOSIS

If the history is accurate and the child holds his arm with palm facing back, the diagnosis is obvious. Attempts to turn the palm forward cause pain. Without history of a yanked arm, diagnosis is more difficult. The most common incorrect diagnosis is that the child has an injured wrist.

HOME TREATMENT

The first time the condition occurs it is best to have a doctor treat it. A dislocated elbow tends to be recurrent, however, and having observed the treatment once, parents can frequently do it themselves.

PRECAUTIONS

● If history does not fit the classical description, do not attempt to reduce the dislocation. A fracture of a forearm bone can produce a similar clinical picture. ● If the elbow is dislocated for more than a few hours, correction may be more difficult because of the swelling, and then for one to two days after correction the arm may still be sore and not fully usable. ● The joint remains susceptible to resubluxation for three to four weeks. Be careful. ● Make a habit of lifting your child under the armpits and not by pulling on hands, wrists, or forearms.

DOCTOR'S TREATMENT

Your doctor will confirm the diagnosis and may require an X ray to rule out fracture. Sometimes, positioning the arm for the X ray results in an inadvertent cure. After the diagnosis is certain, your doctor will reduce the subluxation.

Earaches

DESCRIPTION

Earaches occur at any age from infancy on, but with decreasing frequency after age eight. Earaches may be: mild or excruciatingly painful; constant or intermittent; or present only with chewing, burping, or nose blowing. They may or may not be accompanied by fever, signs of head cold, or diminished hearing.

The most common cause of an earache is blockage of the eustachian tube (which connects the nose with the middle ear), the result of a nasal allergy, a head cold, infected adenoids, and swimming in fresh or chlorinated water. This blockage causes the formation of a vacuum in the middle ear, pressure changes on the eardrum, and secretion of fluid into the airspace of the middle ear. If obstruction of the eustachian tube persists, infection of the middle ear with pus formation (otitis media) may develop promptly. If the eardrum ruptures, ear discharge develops.

An earache may result from foreign objects in the ear canal, impacted earwax, or from pain in the jaw or molar teeth. Boils may develop in the ear canal from scratching or digging in the ear with bobby pins, hair pins, fingernails, or cotton swabs.

Complications of untreated middle ear infections include mastoiditis, meningitis, and perforated and draining ear. Both middle and outer ear infections can cause swollen, tender lymph nodes.

DIAGNOSIS

If your child is too young to communicate the location of pain, prolonged crying should always be suspected as signifying earache. This is particularly so if the infant has a head cold or congested nose, pulls on his ear, or has recently gone swimming.

The pain of an obstructed eustachian tube is apt to be intermittent, low-grade, and affected by chewing or swallowing. Progression to an abscessed middle ear (otitis media) usually causes intense, often throbbing pain. If the eardrum ruptures, pain quickly abates.

The pain from an infection in the canal, a boil in the canal, a foreign body, or impacted cerumen (earwax) is mild at first and gradually builds.

HOME TREATMENT

Any ear pain can be temporarily controlled by aspirin or acetaminophen. Gentle heat applied to the ear may relieve pain but occasionally worsens it. Anesthetic ear drops must penetrate to the eardrum, and some ear, nose, and throat doctors prefer that they not be used. Nose drops and oral decongestants may open the eustachian tube for an earache accompanied by nasal congestion or allergy.

PRECAUTIONS

● Children with congested noses should not go swimming ● Early treatment of head colds and nasal allergies with nose drops and oral decongestants may prevent some ear problems. ● Children susceptible to swimmer's ear

continued

should have their ear canals cleaned by a doctor at the start of each season and preventive ear drops instilled at the end of each swimming day. ● Persistent (more than a few hours) and severe earaches should be seen by your doctor.

DOCTOR'S TREATMENT

The cause of pain will be established by careful inspection of your child's ears, nose, throat, and neck. For otitis media, your doctor will prescribe antibiotics by mouth for five to ten days or until the ear is normal. Nose drops, oral decongestants, and anti-allergy medications also may be prescribed.

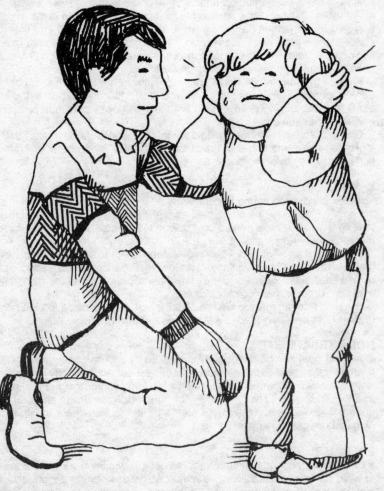

Earaches can be excruciatingly painful.

Encephalitis

DESCRIPTION

Encephalitis is an inflammation of the brain. The causes are innumerable and include poisons, bacteria, vaccines, and parasites. But most cases are caused by viruses, many of which are familiar in relation to such diseases as mumps, measles, rubella, chicken pox, herpes, mononucleosis, hepatitis, and influenza. The whooping cough bacterium can cause encephalitis, as can the vaccines used to prevent whooping cough, measles, influenza, rabies, yellow fever, and typhoid. The vaccines are far less likely to cause encephalitis, however, than are the illnesses they prevent. Lead, mercury, and other poisons also may cause encephalitis.

Encephalitis may start with the symptoms of a common cold. Either no fever or a high fever (105°F) may be present. The child usually has a headache, vomits, and is disoriented and sleepy. Occasionally convulsions and unconsciousness may occur.

DIAGNOSIS

If a recognizable disease is present (measles, mumps, whooping cough) symptoms of encephalitis may occur as a complication of the primary illness. History of exposure to poisons may arouse suspicions.

The most clear-cut physical indication of encephalitis is a stiff neck. A child with the condition will be unable to flex his neck forward to touch his chest with his chin while his mouth is closed. Sometimes the child cannot sit up without supporting himself with both hands braced behind him in tripod fashion. **This is a life-threatening situation.**

HOME TREATMENT

None. See your doctor.

PRECAUTIONS

● If your child has a severe reaction to any of the vaccines listed above, be sure to tell your doctor before a booster of the vaccine is given.

DOCTOR'S TREATMENT

Hospitalization may be required. Diagnosis is made on the basis of history; spinal tap; blood count; recovery of organism from spinal fluid, nose, throat, and stools; and upon the presence of antibodies in the patient's blood. There is specific treatment available for only a few types.

Eye Injuries

DESCRIPTION

The eye can be injured by small objects like sand or metallic splinters that land on or become embedded in the surface or that penetrate to the inside of the eye. Sharp objects, such as fingernails, knives, and fishhooks, can scratch the surface and penetrate the eye. Dull objects, such as squash balls and baseball bats, can jar the eye and dislodge its internal structures. A tiny speck in the eye may lodge on the surface or hide under the lid.

DIAGNOSIS

When the eyeball is injured, the pain often will cause the victim to involuntarily close his eyelids tightly; light may be painful. The eye must be scrupulously examined to determine the seriousness of the damage. If your child cannot easily open his eye for examination, do not attempt to force it open; any damage may be compounded. See your doctor promptly.

If your child can open his eye, look carefully for all of the following: free blood coming from the eyeball (do not be misled by blood from a cut near the eye that may have run into the eye); any differences in the pupil of the affected eye compared to the good eye (larger? smaller? different color?); any difference in the color or position of the iris (colored part of the eye); any sign of collapse of the eyeball; puddling of red blood in front of the iris; and blurring of vision. (If present, see below.) If none of these is present you may safely look for objects adherent to eyeball or lodged under lid.

HOME TREATMENT

If any of the above signs is present, place a soft bandage over the eye and **see your doctor promptly.** If none of the above signs is present and you see a speck on the eyeball or under the lid (and the child is cooperative) you may try to remove the speck by gentle strokes with a cotton swab. In older children, an eye cup may be used. If the speck does not immediately come off, stop. The object may be embedded. **See a doctor.**

PRECAUTIONS

● The eyeball is delicate and invaluable. Be cautious about treating eye injuries yourself. ● **If a harmful liquid or powder enters the eye** (acids, alkalis, caustics, gasoline), **immediate action is imperative. Seconds count!** Hold the eye open and flush it with pints of cool water. If possible put your child into a cool shower, clothes and all, and wash out his eye. Then, immediately take child to your doctor for further care. ● Do not attempt to remove a fishhook or any other object that has penetrated the eye. ● Some golf balls explode and cause eye injuries if they are unwound. ● **Beware!** Carbon dioxide cartridges and spray cans explode violently in fires. Be sure your child knows this. ● Machine sanders, paint removers, and grindstones throw off particles. Protective glasses and supervision are essential to protect your child's eyes.

DOCTOR'S TREATMENT

A doctor can easily anesthetize the eye and examine it internally and externally without pain or damage.

Fainting

DESCRIPTION

Fainting is a temporary loss of consciousness caused by the involuntary (autonomic) nervous system. It can be initiated by pain, physical fatigue, low blood sugar, a disturbing scene, sudden fright, and other strong emotions. The child experiences light-headedness, narrowing of visual fields, clamminess, and sometimes mild nausea just before unconsciousness. An observer may notice a paleness or "green color" and a glazed look in the eyes at the onset of a faint. Occasionally there will be mild, convulsive movements while the child is unconscious. Rarely will control of the urine or stools be lost. Consciousness will be recovered within a few minutes and the child will probably not remember the event.

Fainting is common in preadolescent and adolescent children. It often occurs after the child has gone without eating for an extended period of time. A partial faint (light-headedness and dizziness) or a complete faint is also common when a teenager abruptly changes position, for example jumping up from a reclining or sitting position.

DIAGNOSIS

Diagnosis is made by consideration of the circumstances, plus a complete, rapid recovery (which suggests it's nothing more serious than an isolated spell). The pulse at the wrist may be diagnostically feeble and slow or not present at all. The heartbeat (ear against chest) is slow, usually 50 beats per minute or slower.

HOME TREATMENT

The only danger in fainting is the injury your child may incur from a fall. Try to catch him as he goes down, and lay him flat on his back, elevating his legs to return the blood to the head. Although not mandatory, the coolness from an open window or air conditioner may help. Keep your child down for five to ten minutes after consciousness returns.

An alternative treatment, if your child is not yet unconscious, is to have him sit with his head between his knees. Place your hand on the back of his head and have him strain to sit up while you hold his head down. This maneuver forces extra blood into the head.

PRECAUTIONS

● Sometimes a first convulsion is mistaken for fainting. If fainting is recurrent or if other signs or epilepsy are present, see your doctor. ● If blueness of skin (cyanosis) is observed during an apparent faint or if your child is not completely well before and after fainting, consult your doctor. Extremely rare heart conditions might simulate fainting.

DOCTOR'S TREATMENT

Your doctor will treat fainting as you would at home. Although fainting cannot be diagnosed after the faint is over, various causes of unconsciousness can be ruled out. Your doctor may require an electrocardiogram, an electroencephalogram, blood chemistries, or a chest X ray.

Fractures

DESCRIPTION

A fracture, a broken bone, and a fractured bone are all the same. Children's bones are still growing, which gives their fractures characteristics that differ from adult fractures. Any deformity caused by a fracture that heals in a poor position tends to be corrected through growth (except if the poor position is one that shortens or rotates the bone). Fractures through the growing cartilage near both ends of long bones may stop growth and cause major deformities. Broken bones heal in less time for children than for adults. All of these traits are even more marked for the very young child.

DIAGNOSIS

Deformity of the bone is visible or can be felt. Pain is aggravated by attempts to move the broken part, and there is a tenderness to pressure that is most severe at the point of the fracture. The function of the fractured part is limited, and there is swelling at the fracture site. Bruising often develops, but sometimes not until days later and in areas many inches from the fracture.

HOME TREATMENT

Protect the injured part. If the arm or shoulder is fractured, the child will usually immobilize the part in the most comfortable position with his other arm. If a leg or spine fracture is suspected, prevent your child from putting weight on the fracture. If splinting is required for your child's arm or leg, a folded pillow is often the best splint. Immobilize the fractured area in a comfortable position and take the child to your doctor.

Obvious fractures usually raise no question of home treatment. Problems arise from borderline cases, as in the following fractures:

Collar bone (clavicle). This is the most common fracture in young children. It occurs from a fall onto the point of the shoulder. There is pain on raising the arm overhead. The entire bone is just beneath the skin, so it can be touched carefully with the fingers to feel the point of tenderness, lump, and change in contour compared to opposite clavicle.

Wrist (lower radius or ulna). This is the most common fracture in older children. It occurs from a fall on an outstretched arm. Unlike with a sprain, the most tender point is usually one-half inch to two inches above the wrist joint. Also unlike a sprain, it hurts the child to turn the palm up and down.

Elbow (lower humerus). Moderate to marked swelling is present and the most tender point is above or at the joint and also along the inside or outside edge of the bone. Any motion of the forearm causes pain.

Ankle (lower femur or fibula). Unless the break is severe, an ankle fracture is hard to differentiate from a sprain. The tender point is above the lower tip of the bone rather than at or below the tip.

Foot (metatarsal bones). The five slender bones that make up the instep are often fractured, sometimes just by marching (march fracture) or running. This type of fracture is extremely difficult to diagnose, and even X rays may be normal until one to two weeks after the fracture occurs.

Toes. Unless there is a great deformity or a compound fracture, diagnosis doesn't matter. Put a wad of cotton between the injured toe and those on either side of it, and bind them together with adhesive tape. The fracture will heal perfectly in two to three weeks.

Fingers. If the fracture occurs in the bone beneath the fingernail (as might be caused by a slammed door or a hammer blow) it will heal perfectly without treatment unless the injury broke the skin. Other finger fractures are serious if the fractured finger is not straight or if the skin is broken. Otherwise, splinting for three to four weeks is sufficient. **If you suspect fracture, take your child to your doctor.**

PRECAUTIONS

● A dangerous, often overlooked fracture is that of the navicular (scaphoid) bone of the wrist. The navicular bone resembles a small cashew nut, is one of eight small bones in the wrist, and lies near the base of the thumb's metacarpal bone. This fracture causes only moderate pain and little swelling, but if it is not treated, part of the bone dies, resulting in a permanent deformity. Any point of tenderness in this area after injury should be seen by a doctor. ● Do not move an injured extremity to conform to a splint. Splint a possible fracture in the position found with a wood lath or a pillow (see Home Treatment). ● Do not move your child if there is any possibility of a neck or spine injury.

DOCTOR'S TREATMENT

Your doctor's treatment will depend largely upon what the X rays show. Open or closed reduction of fracture will be performed with casting or mechanical pinning if necessary.

A child's broken bone will heal more rapidly than will an adult's.

Gastroenteritis, Acute

DESCRIPTION

Acute gastroenteritis is a highly contagious infection of the digestive tract that is probably caused by viruses, only a few of which have been identified. There is evidence indicating that the disease may also be caused by some types of bacteria.

Acute gastroenteritis causes a sudden onset of vomiting or diarrhea and cramps. The disease lasts one to three days, sometimes a week. Fever may be high (104°F), low (101°F), or absent. Blood in diarrhea is rare. Occasionally, there are small amounts of blood in vomitus and petechiae (red spots) of the face if vomiting is severe. The disease is readily transmitted from person to person. The incubation period is one to four days. The disease is not generally serious except in young babies, who may become dehydrated. One attack confers variable, brief, or no immunity against subsequent attacks. Acute gastroenteritis has no relationship to true flu, a disease of the respiratory tract.

DIAGNOSIS

Acute gastroenteritis is usually obvious if there are other cases in the family or neighborhood. It occasionally must be distinguished from dysentery and food poisoning.

HOME TREATMENT

Treat vomiting and diarrhea. Limit food intake to clear liquids until the illness subsides. Give acetaminophen for relief of fever.

PRECAUTIONS

● If illness is present in siblings, isolate a baby in a room with a closed door.
● Practice good hygiene. Be sure to wash your hands before going from the patient to a baby. ● If a young child develops the disease, watch carefully for signs of dehydration.

DOCTOR'S TREATMENT

Your doctor will confirm the diagnosis by knowledge of what illnesses are current in the community, by history, and by absence of other physical findings on examination. Blood count and a stool culture might be required if diagnosis is in doubt. Otherwise, your doctor's treatment will be the same as home treatment. If there is evidence of dehydration in an infant, hospitalization may be necessary in order to administer intravenous fluids.

Growing Pains

DESCRIPTION

Growing pains refers to a popular concept that is half truth and half myth. Growing children do have "normal" pains, particularly in their legs and feet, but they are not caused by growing. They are caused by excessive use of the immature young muscles and joints and the exuberance of youth. These pains can be quite severe and typically occur in the thighs, calves, and feet, and can awaken a child from sleep.

DIAGNOSIS

The identifying characteristic of growing pains is that they only occur at rest—usually at night or during naps. They never occur when the child is active, which is the time that pain from most disease or abnormalities is worse. The pain does not interfere with or interrupt a child's daily play or routine, and fever or other systemic symptoms are never present.

HOME TREATMENT

Love, sympathy, local application of heat, massage, and aspirin or acetaminophen are advised. Sometimes sturdier shoes reduce the frequency and severity of growing pains.

PRECAUTIONS

● If your child complains of a frequent, nightly pain that is always in the same spot, the cause must be checked by your doctor.

DOCTOR'S TREATMENT

Your doctor will perform a careful examination to rule out other diseases. X rays may be necessary.

A gentle massage of the affected area can ease sore muscles.

Gynecomastia

DESCRIPTION

Gynecomastia is the development of breasts in a boy. Normal males have rudimentary breast tissue, which can become enlarged by estrogens (female hormones) and rarely by androgens (male hormones). A boy with tumors of the testes or adrenal glands may develop appreciable breasts. Rarely, the same situation can occur from mistakenly ingesting sex hormones as medication or from eating poultry fattened by hormones.

Normal adolescent boys commonly develop small breasts on one or both sides. These persist for two to twenty-four months, may be tender, and are often an embarrassment. The breasts may become quite pronounced and remain for years, but this is not common. Obese boys may develop large fat accumulations that resemble breasts (pseudogynecomastia) but that contain no true breast tissue.

DIAGNOSIS

The diagnosis is obvious except when boys try to hide gynecomastia out of embarrassment. If this happens, the parent may not be aware of the problem.

HOME TREATMENT

Understanding and reassurance, especially from a male relative or friend, are very important. In more obvious cases the boy may need to take activities in physical education that do not require undressing or showering with others.

PRECAUTIONS

• Ninety-eight percent of the cases of gynecomastia are normal and will disappear spontaneously. • Your doctor should have an opportunity to examine your boy if the condition persists. • Taunting by siblings must be firmly forbidden.

DOCTOR'S TREATMENT

Your doctor will examine your boy carefully, feeling for the presence or absence of true breast tissue, checking the coloration of areolae (nipples), and investigating abdominal or testicular masses and the distribution of sexual hair. A careful history of drug and food ingestion will be taken. If other causes of the condition are ruled out, your doctor can only recommend your patience and support, and counseling. Hormonal studies or chromosome studies are rarely needed. In severe or prolonged cases, plastic surgery can remove breast tissue without visible scarring.

Gynecomastia calls for a man's understanding and support.

Hand, Foot, & Mouth Disease

DESCRIPTION

Hand, foot, and mouth disease is a common, easily recognizable, contagious illness caused by the coxsackie viruses. The disease is prevalent during warm weather and the average incubation period is three to five days. It is transmitted by mouth-to-mouth contact with someone who has the disease or by ingestion of fecally contaminated material.

The disease is characterized by blisters and sores in the mouth (cheeks, tongue, lips, throat) resembling canker sores, plus small, clear blisters (one-sixteenth to one-eighth inch round) on the fingers, hands, toes, and feet. Fever may be absent, low (101°F), or high (104°F). Sometimes there is a viral rash on the skin. The illness lasts three to seven days.

DIAGNOSIS

Typical appearance of the above symptoms is diagnostic. Other types of coxsackie illnesses in the family or among your child's friends are suggestive of the disease.

HOME TREATMENT

Give acetaminophen for fever and soreness of the mouth. Avoid foods that sting the mouth, such as citrus juices, ginger ale, and spices. Administer antihistamines according to your doctor's directions if needed for the itchiness of blisters and rash.

PRECAUTIONS

● This disease occasionally **can be dangerous for young infants.** Isolate babies from ill siblings. ● If your infant contracts this disease, report it to your doctor.

DOCTOR'S TREATMENT

Your doctor's treatment is the same as home treatment. Rarely will hospitalization of an ill and toxic infant for supportive therapy (relief of pain, intravenous feeding, etc.) be necessary.

Acetaminophen will reduce fever and relieve soreness.

Hay Fever

DESCRIPTION

Hay fever is an allergic reaction of the membranes of the nose and sinuses to inhaled substances. When it occurs only during a particular time of the year (seasonal), hay fever is usually due to pollens of trees, grasses, or weeds. (Pollens of flowers are usually too heavy to be airborne or inhaled and are therefore seldom responsible.) When hay fever occurs year round (perennial), it may be due to dander from a cat, dog, horse, or cow (present in some felt underpaddings of carpetings) but rarely from guinea pigs, hamsters, gerbils, and mice. Feathers (from pillows, comforters, and pet birds), house dust, and molds can also be responsible. Hay fever is rarely due to foods, beverages, or medications.

Symptoms are nasal congestion, sneezing, clear nasal discharge, and itching of the nose. The eyes also may be involved. A headache results from involvement of sinuses. The ears feel obstructed and are sometimes painful, and hearing is diminished due to the obstruction of the eustachian tubes. Bluish bags under the eyes, called "allergic shiners," may be present. Your child may snore and complain of fatigue (allergic fatigue syndrome). In addition, secondary bacterial infections are common.

DIAGNOSIS

Membranes inside the nose are pale and white instead of the normal pink in the presence of hay fever. Prompt, temporary relief from oral antihistamines strengthens the diagnosis. Development of fever, moderate to severe earache, swollen glands in the neck, or opaque (green, yellow, or milky) nasal discharge indicates secondary infection.

HOME TREATMENT

Consult your doctor concerning medications. Oral antihistamines may provide relief. Reduce the child's exposure to offending substances (antigens) whenever possible. (The dander of a cat or dog allowed in the house only once a month can remain in the home for four to six weeks.) Keep the windows closed against pollens, and use an air conditioner if possible. Hot air ducts should have filters at room inlets to minimize dust. Use nonallergenic pillows and dehumidify the house.

PRECAUTIONS

• Rubber pillows, which are considered nonallergenic, may breed molds as they age. • Avoid repeated use of decongestant nose drops, which can cause worse congestion following the initial, brief relief.

DOCTOR'S TREATMENT

In addition to home treatment, your doctor can help identify the offending substance by taking the child's history and, if necessary, conducting allergy skin tests. He will substantiate the diagnosis by the appearance of the nose and by taking a smear of nasal secretions, which will reveal allergic white blood cells. Nasal spray may be prescribed. Your doctor will rarely recommend oral steroids for a brief period or desensitization shots for years for severe cases.

Headaches

DESCRIPTION

Headaches are probably as common in children as in adults and have as many or more causes. Fever and strong emotions (anxiety, fear, excitement, sadness, and worry) account for 95 percent of all headaches. Less common causes are high blood pressure (hypertension), head injuries and concussions, tumors and infections of the brain (meningitis, encephalitis), bleeding inside skull, sinusitis, eye strain, psychiatric problems, and epilepsy.

DIAGNOSIS

The diagnosis depends in large part upon a carefully detailed history and response to medications. In general, a headache that responds to aspirin or acetaminophen—plus love—is not serious.

Migraine. A child who has a migraine usually has a strong family history of the condition. The headache is often one-sided and is generally accompanied by nausea and vomiting ("sick headache") and sometimes is preceded by an aura (seeing light flashes, or double vision, etc.) It is most common in high achievers and self-motivated children. A migraine lasts for hours and usually responds poorly to aspirin or acetaminophen.

Hypertension. A throbbing pain occurs with the headache associated with hypertension. The child may sweat and turn pale or become flushed; heart and pulse pound. There is no relief with aspirin or acetaminophen.

Concussions. A concussion is diagnosed by history and other accompanying signs.

Tumor, infections, intracranial bleeding. Headaches associated with these illnesses become increasingly more severe and frequent. Vomiting and other neurological signs (stiff neck, visual problems, disorientation, loss of balance, and sometimes fever) develop.

Sinusitis. The nose is obstructed or runny when a child has sinusitis. Other signs of allergic rhinitis or infection are present. Antihistamines or nose drops may offer relief.

Eye strain. A headache from eye strain is never present while sleeping or upon arising. It parallels reading or watching television.

Psychiatric problems. Behavior problems are also present when a headache is caused by psychiatric problems. The headache is frequently at the top of the head or may affect the entire head, which is unusual with other forms of headache.

HOME TREATMENT

Try aspirin, acetaminophen, antihistamines, or nose drops. Try reassurance, cuddling, and cold compresses. Lay the child down in a dark room. Try to remove any major family or school pressure from your child. If the headache persists, see your doctor.

PRECAUTIONS

• Sudden, severe headache—especially with fever, prostration, violent vomiting, disorientation or stiff neck—may be a **true emergency.** Get imme-

continued

diate, competent, professional advice. ● Headaches that recur with increasing frequency and severity may be serious. See your doctor promptly. ● Headaches with other neurological signs are almost always serious. See your doctor. ● Investigation for cause of headaches may be simple or extremely complicated, but diagnosis depends heavily upon an accurate history. Observe the location of the pain, its duration, the time of day, the circumstances that provoke it, accompanying symptoms, and response to medications. Report these to your doctor.

DOCTOR'S TREATMENT

Your doctor will perform a complete physical examination of your child, including measuring the blood pressure and examining the eyes (plus a neurological examination). Tests indicated are numerous and dictated by history and examination.

Consultation with a neurologist; allergist; ear, nose, and throat doctor; or psychiatrist may be required. Your doctor also may prescribe diagnostic trials of ergotamine and phenobarbital for a migraine. In perplexing cases your doctor can refer your child to a headache diagnostic clinic at a medical center.

Cuddling and cold compresses can help your child's headache.

Head Lice

DESCRIPTION

Head lice are tiny parasites (smaller than fleas) less than one-eighth inch in length. They are grayish-white, almost transparent creatures with six legs. They live exclusively on humans, never on pets. They pass from one human to another and live on or close to the scalp, where they bite and suck blood. Their visible eggs, which stick to the hairs, are milk-white and about the size of a flake of dandruff.

Head lice cause itching of the scalp and sometimes a red, scaly rash on the back of the neck at the hairline. Because of scratching, sores of the scalp may develop. The lymph nodes at the base of the skull may be enlarged. During the past few years, infestation with head lice has become common among school-age children.

DIAGNOSIS

Unless hundreds are present, it is difficult to see lice in a child's hair. Look for the small but easily visible eggs (called nits) attached to the shafts of the hairs. Nits are readily distinguished from flakes of dandruff, which can be blown or brushed away; nits can scarcely be detached with fingernails.

HOME TREATMENT

Apply two tablespoonfuls of a one percent gamma-benzene hexachloride shampoo (available by prescription) to your child's dry hair, work it into a lather, leave it on four minutes, then rinse. This kills both the lice and the eggs. Fine-comb your child's hair to remove the nits. If necessary, a vinegar rinse will loosen the nits. Repeat the procedure once, four to seven days later. Clean combs and hairbrushes with gamma-benzene hexachloride shampoo. Clean hats and pillowcases by washing and ironing or by dry-cleaning to kill stray lice.

Lice can also be killed by the application of a 25 percent benzyl benzoate lotion (available over-the-counter) to the hair and scalp; shampoo after 12 to 24 hours. Repeat the procedure in four to seven days.

PRECAUTIONS

● **Gamma-benzene hexachloride** is lindane, a white powder used chiefly as an insecticide, and **is poisonous** if swallowed or absorbed through the skin. Do not leave it within your child's reach. Do not apply it more than twice. ● If one person has head lice carefully check the heads of all other family members for evidence of infestation. ● If there are infected sores of the scalp or enlarged tender glands at the base of the skull consult your doctor.

DOCTOR'S TREATMENT

Your doctor will treat head lice as you would at home. If there are infected sores and infected lymph nodes your doctor may culture the sores and will usually prescribe an oral antibiotic for five to ten days.

Heat Rash

DESCRIPTION

Heat rash is the most common of all rashes in children of any age. Also known as prickly heat or miliaria, it is almost universal in babies during hot weather; heat rash can even occur in a cold climate if your child is overdressed during the day or at nighttime. Fair-skinned children (redheads and blonds) are the most frequent sufferers of heat rash, and they suffer the most from it. Usual locations are cheeks, neck, shoulders, skin creases, and diaper area. It frequently appears under wet bathing trunks.

Heat rash consists of hundreds of tiny pinhead eruptions, each surrounding a skin pore. Those elements may be small, pink or red bumps or tiny water blisters. They are moderately itchy and may show scratch marks.

DIAGNOSIS

History of exposure to hot, humid conditions, perspiration, and overdressing are diagnostic clues. Diagnosis is confirmed by inspection of the rash with a magnifying glass in good light. Each dot of heat rash is seen at the mouth of a pore representing a sweat gland.

HOME TREATMENT

Keep your child as cool as possible. If the heat rash is on your baby's face, rest his face on an absorbent pad in the crib. Infants and children are safest from heat rash in an air-conditioned environment. Giving cool baths and sponging your child with diluted rubbing alcohol help. Baby powder or cornstarch applied lightly with a powder puff also helps. During warm weather, the use of prickly heat powders may give some relief. Give antihistamines by mouth if itching is intense.

PRECAUTIONS

● Detergents and bleaches in clothing and bed linens may aggravate heat rash. ● Bubble baths, water softeners, and oily cosmetics should be avoided.

DOCTOR'S TREATMENT

None.

*A dusting of baby powder or cornstarch
may provide some relief from heat rash.*

Hernia

DESCRIPTION

A hernia, or rupture, is a protrusion of tissue through the wall of a body cavity. It might be compared to the protrusion of an inner tube through a hole in a bicycle tire.

The most common hernia in a child is an *indirect inguinal hernia,* present but not always detectable at birth. Usually, this form of hernia doesn't become apparent until some later age. It begins as a bulge just above the midpoint of the crease of the groin. It then enlarges toward the midline until it reaches and enters the scrotum of a boy or the labia majora of a girl. The bulge consists of a subcutaneous sac (peritoneum), which contains a portion of the omentum (a veil-like apron that overlies the intestines) or a loop of the small intestine. Less often, it contains a loop of the large bowel, urinary bladder, or ovary.

A rarer site is below the crease of the groin near where the pulse of the main artery to the leg can be felt. This is a *femoral hernia.* Infrequently, a true hernia appears in the midline of the abdomen above or below the navel as a *ventral hernia.* Frequently, a herniation is present at the umbilicus of infants and is called an *umbilical hernia.* This is not a true hernia, however, because it contains no sac, and it usually disappears spontaneously before age five.

DIAGNOSIS

Diagnosis is made by the typical location and by noting that the contents of the sac can be pushed gently back (reduced) into the abdominal cavity. If a hernia cannot be reduced, it is said to be incarcerated. If the blood supply to the contents of the hernia is cut off, it is said to be strangulated. A strangulated hernia causes intense pain and swelling. Simple and incarcerated hernias produce no symptoms or merely a sense of heaviness.

HOME TREATMENT

A hernia can be temporarily reduced by gentle pressure while the child is relaxed—in a warm tub, if necessary. Trusses and belts to keep a hernia reduced are useless and may be harmful or even dangerous. Strapping an umbilical hernia is now considered of no benefit.

PRECAUTIONS

● Strangulation of a hernia, with accompanying severe pain and sometimes nausea, vomiting, and prostration, is a **medical emergency** that requires immediate (within hours) surgical correction. ● Never attempt to reduce a strangulated hernia that has been present for more than a few minutes.

DOCTOR'S TREATMENT

Surgical repair is required for all except umbilical hernias. An umbilical hernia usually cures itself. Although opinions vary as to the best time to correct a persistent umbilical hernia, the range is generally set from age two to age five or later. Since hernias often appear on both sides, the surgeon may correct both sides even though only one side is visibly herniated.

Herpes Simplex

DESCRIPTION

Herpes simplex is a highly contagious disease caused by herpesvirus hominis, types 1 and 2. Commonly called canker sores (in the mouth) or fever blisters (near the mouth), herpes simplex is transmitted by direct contact.

Infection with type 1 is common before age four but may occur at any age. It causes many painful ulcers of the membranes of the mouth (lips, cheeks, tongue, palate) and eyeballs; gums are red, swollen, and painful; the child's temperature may reach as high as 105°F; lymph nodes in the neck swell. The condition lasts seven to ten days. After the symptoms disappear, the virus continues to live in the body for months, years, or even throughout the individual's lifetime. When resistance is lowered by such conditions as fever, sunburn, exhaustion, or emotional stress, the "sleeping" virus is re-activated; and isolated, painful ulcers appear in or near the mouth or in a closely packed collection of small blisters on the skin. These are recurrent herpes and are also contagious.

Infection with type 2 herpesvirus hominis causes painful ulcers and blisters on the genitalia (labia, vagina, cervix, or penis). As with oral herpes, genital herpes is contagious and often recurrent. If a baby is delivered via the birth canal of a mother with genital herpes, he or she can contract a generalized and overwhelming infection of herpesvirus and has a fifty percent chance of severe, permanent damage or death.

DIAGNOSIS

The initial attack of herpes simplex is accompanied by fever, ulcers of the mouth, and swollen gums. Subsequent canker sores appear as open, red ulcers of the mouth that are unique in appearance. Gum boils protrude above the surface of the membranes; canker sores have a scooped-out appearance. Fever blisters are easily mistaken for impetigo but are generally more painful. To confuse the diagnosis, fever blisters may become secondarily infected with impetigo.

HOME TREATMENT

Control pain and fever with acetaminophen. Give bland, soothing foods, such as ice cream, gelatin desserts, puddings, and milk. An older child may rinse his mouth with mild sodium perborate or table salt solutions. Canker sores can be treated with local anesthetics available in brand-name form at your pharmacy. Application of antibiotic ointment to fever blisters may prevent painful cracking and stop impetigo from taking hold.

PRECAUTIONS

● Herpes simplex of the eyeball is serious. See your eye doctor promptly. ● Herpes can be severe in an infant. Keep siblings and adults with herpes from contact with the baby. See your doctor.

DOCTOR'S TREATMENT

Your doctor will prescribe eyedrops for herpes of the eyeball. A child with a severely ulcerated mouth may require hospitalization and intravenous fluids until he is able to swallow liquids.

If a mother who is about to deliver has genital herpes, a Cesarean section may be performed within four hours of the rupture of maternal membranes to avoid exposing the baby to the disease. The newborn must then be isolated from the mother.

There is no way to eradicate recurrent herpes. Repeated smallpox vaccinations and injections of vitamins are not effective and may be harmful.

Apply antibiotic ointment to fever blisters to prevent cracking.

Hives

DESCRIPTION

Hives (urticaria) are an allergic reaction of the skin. Hives appear as red, itchy, raised welts that range in size from one-fourth-inch to several inches in diameter. Twenty percent of children have hives once or repeatedly. Hives may involve any area of skin. They often result in huge swelling of the genitalia and swelling of the lips of the mouth. Their most characteristic aspect is their rapidly changing appearance—hives come and go and change size hourly.

Ninety-five percent of the cases are caused by ingestion of foods, beverages, or medications to which the child is allergic. Citrus fruits, chocolate, nuts (peanut butter), tomatoes, berries, spices, candies, tropical fruits (juices), and artificial flavorings are particular offenders. The remaining five percent of cases are caused by something the child has come in contact with (e.g., plants, ointments, cosmetics, dog and cat saliva), insect bites and stings, excessive exposure to the sun or cold, or inhalants (e.g., pollens, insecticides, molds, animal dander, feathers). An unusual form of hives is caused by respiratory and other viruses, medications, and streptococcus. This form is called *erythema multiforme* and looks like different-sized red targets painted on the skin. Hives sometimes cause allergic arthritis.

DIAGNOSIS

All welts that itch and rapidly change appearance are hives. No other rash has these traits.

HOME TREATMENT

To pinpoint the cause consider your child's activities during the minutes or hours preceding the onset of hives. Oral antihistamines usually work well and may have to be continued for up to a week if hives recur. Cold applications, calamine lotion, and cornstarch baths may be of some help.

PRECAUTIONS

● If hives involve the tongue, or cause a cough or difficulty in breathing or swallowing, see your doctor **immediately.** ● If hives are accompanied by fever, see your doctor to rule out strep infections. ● If antihistamines don't help, telephone your doctor for advice.

DOCTOR'S TREATMENT

Your doctor may administer bronchodilators, decongestants, steroids, or antihistamines if the case is severe. Oral steroids will be tried if antihistamines are ineffective. If hives are recurrent and the cause is not clear from your child's history, your doctor may perform skin tests or refer your child to an allergist. A throat culture may be ordered to check for strep infection. If symptoms of arthritis are present, your doctor may order tests for confirmation of the disorder. If hives are caused by insects, your doctor will probably suggest a long-term course (years) of desensitizing shots. In such a case your child should carry medications with him to take if he is stung.

Hyperactivity

DESCRIPTION

All healthy children are active. Most are more active, at least part of the time, than a sedate adult would prefer, and some are very active. Of these active children only one to ten percent have true hyperkinesis, a condition in which (under most circumstances) they are unable to be quiet and motionless for more than a few moments.

Hyperactivity (hyperkinesis) is part of the clinical picture described as minimal brain dysfunction (MBD). Other symptoms that may be present in any combination are: poor coordination (clumsiness), emotional outbursts, lack of concentration, and learning disabilities. Hyperactivity may be due to late or faulty development of the brain centers whose functions are to filter incoming stimuli (sights, sounds, smells, touches, tastes) and to regulate self-control. Behavior that closely mimics hyperactivity is seen in children with normal brain centers, but whose centers were never stimulated or taught. Children raised in total permissiveness or neglect may have such untutored control centers.

DIAGNOSIS

Hyperactivity is fairly obvious in extreme cases: the child is constantly in physical motion. This behavior is annoying and often destructive, but not malicious. The child cannot sit still to be read to or to watch television for more than a few seconds or minutes.

Most cases are less severe and consequently more difficult to diagnose. Check with school officials and your physician concerning your child's legal right to evaluation and treatment. Testing by a trained psychologist is often necessary. Neurological examination and an electroencephalogram are universally recommended by non-medical professionals (e.g. educators), but rarely are of diagnostic help. An experienced neurologist may recognize a hyperkinetic child at a glance.

HOME TREATMENT

Home treatment is limited without professional advice. Once professional advice has been obtained, home treatment is of great importance, but only as it is tailored to a particular child's needs. Caffeine sometimes lessens hyperkinesis, but is not advised without professional recommendation. The avoidance of all foods with artificial colorings, flavorings, and preservatives is reputed to help. However, the special attention required to maintain such a diet may account for any improvement in the child's behavior.

PRECAUTIONS

● True hyperactivity is present from infancy. If your normally behaved child suddenly becomes overactive past the age of one or two years, look for clues in the child's environment. ● If your child is overactive with one parent and not with the other, the child does not have hyperkinesis. ● Only accept a decision concerning hyperactivity from an experienced, trained, and skilled professional. Accurate diagnosis often requires a team approach.

continued

DOCTOR'S TREATMENT

Your doctor will give a complete physical and neurological examination, including vision and hearing tests. A careful and detailed history will be taken, and school reports will be evaluated. A battery of tests by a psychologist (psychometrics) will generally be recommended. Your doctor may try a diagnostic or therapeutic trial of medications and will require accurate follow-up reports from parents and teachers regarding any changes in your child's behavior. The hyperkinetic child will often need special educational facilities and sometimes psychiatric counseling for any emotional problems that are secondary to his poor family, peer, and school relationships.

The truly hyperactive child cannot sit still.

Impetigo

DESCRIPTION

Impetigo is a highly contagious infection of the superficial layers of the skin. It is caused by staphylococcus and/or streptococcus germs. It is transmitted by direct contact with infected persons or objects such as clothing, towels, toys, and sandboxes. The incubation period is two to five days.

Impetigo typically starts as a fragile blister containing thin, yellow pus. The blister is easily broken, leaving an open, weeping sore that increases in size. The discharge hardens into a yellow crust or scab and readily spreads the disease to other areas of the skin. The initial sore is often at the point of injured skin, which has been irritated by an insect bite, scrape, poison ivy, eczema, or (around the nostrils) from picking the nose. If the infecting germ is caused by streptococcus, glomerulonephritis—a kidney complication— may develop.

DIAGNOSIS

Rapidly spreading, moist sores that form crusts that resemble hardened honey are characteristic of impetigo. Any open wound that fails to heal promptly should suggest impetigo. Distinction between streptococcal and staphylococcal infection can be made only by a culture.

HOME TREATMENT

If only a few small areas are involved, remove the crusts of the lesions by softening them with soap and water. (Streptococcal and staphylococcal infections thrive *under* the crusts.) Apply an antibiotic ointment several times daily. Cover the sores with gauze to keep the ointment in place and to discourage your child from scratching and spreading the disease.

PRECAUTIONS

● Treat minor scratches and scrapes with soap and water and a sterile bandage to avoid impetigo. ● If your child has impetigo, watch the rest of the family carefully and treat cases promptly if they occur. ● Keep the wash cloth, towel, and clothing used by a child with impetigo separate from others' items to reduce the chance of spreading it. Ordinary laundering adequately sterilizes clothing. ● If home treatment is not promptly effective, see your doctor. ● Do not discontinue treatment that is working until the sores are completely healed and the skin is smooth. Eradication may require extended treatment.

DOCTOR'S TREATMENT

Your doctor may culture sores and prescribe penicillin for ten to fourteen days if streptococcal infection is present. Sensitivity tests on a staphylococcal infection may be required to determine the most effective antibiotic.

Infectious Mononucleosis

DESCRIPTION

Infectious mononucleosis is a common, contagious disease caused by Epstein-Barr (EB) virus. It most often occurs among those of secondary-school and college age, but it can occur at any age from infancy on. The disease is transmitted via droplets from the nose and throat; it is popularly known as "the kissing disease." The incubation period is one to six weeks, long enough to have forgotten whom you kissed.

The usual symptoms of "mono" are malaise, sore throat, prolonged fever, and a generalized swelling of the lymph glands, which are barely or not at all tender. Ten to twenty percent of the cases have a nonspecific, red, mottled rash, especially on the trunk. Acute illness may last for weeks; fatigue and weakness may go on for months. Complications of mono are hepatitis, ruptured spleen, encephalitis, and spontaneous bleeding (purpura).

DIAGNOSIS

Because mono symptoms suggest other diseases, diagnosis is rarely possible without laboratory tests. Fever, severe sore throat (often with pus or gray membrane on the tonsils), swollen neck glands, and rash may suggest strep throat, tonsillitis, or diphtheria. However, the failure of the symptoms to improve with time and treatment raises the suspicion of mononucleosis. Complications like encephalitis or hepatitis with jaundice may make the diagnosis more difficult.

HOME TREATMENT

Rest, acetaminophen, and diet as tolerated are indicated. If the spleen is enlarged, your child should be prevented from participating in contact sports or other violent activity until the spleen returns to its normal size to avoid rupture. This may take weeks or months. (An enlarged spleen protrudes beneath the ribs, which normally protect it; and it is vulnerable to injury and rupture.) Although mono is contagious, isolation is not required. Your child may return to school as soon as weakness and fatigue subside. Secondary cases in a family are rare.

PRECAUTIONS

● Ten to twenty percent of the cases of mono have a positive throat culture for streptococcal infection for which antiobiotic therapy is required. If your child, ill and with a positive throat culture, does not improve promptly (within 24 to 48 hours) in response to the prescribed antibiotic, report to your doctor so that tests for infectious mononucleosis can be done.

DOCTOR'S TREATMENT

Your doctor will give your child a complete physical examination including evaluation of the liver, spleen, and all lymph node sites. Your doctor also will perform a throat culture and other tests. If the throat culture is positive for streptococcal infection, penicillin or other antibiotic therapy is indicated. Severe cases require hospitalization for the administration of intravenous fluids, possible transfusions, and supportive treatment.

Influenza

DESCRIPTION

Any viral infection of the upper respiratory tract is apt to be referred to as "flu," particularly if it is accompanied by chills, fever, cough, and muscle aches. Influenza is, however, a highly contagious, *specific* respiratory infection that occurs in epidemics and is caused by the influenza A or influenza B virus. It is transmitted by droplets from nose and throat discharges of persons who have the disease. It has a short incubation period of one to three days.

The symptoms are: sudden chills, a sharp rise in body temperature to 102°F to 106°F (sometimes with convulsions), flushing, headache, sore throat, a hacking cough, redness of the eyes, and pains in the back and limbs. In young children, vomiting and diarrhea may occur. Fever lasts three to four days and is followed by days of weakness and fatigue, during which the child is vulnerable to other illnesses.

Secondary bacterial complications are responsible for many of the serious outcomes of flu, and their presence is suggested by: the return of high fever after the third or fourth day of normal temperature; progressive worsening of the cough, changing from dry and hacking to loose and productive; formation of pus in the eyes or a change in nasal discharge from clear to thick and yellow; rapid breathing and shortness of breath beyond that expected from the fever; severe earache; stiff neck; disorientation; and the onset of prostration.

DIAGNOSIS

Isolated cases of influenza cannot be diagnosed with certainty by ordinary tests or on physical examination. During an epidemic, the disease is diagnosed by similarity to other cases. Specific tests for influenza viruses require the use of special laboratory facilities.

HOME TREATMENT

The "prescription" for home care includes bed rest during the height of the fever, acetaminophen for fever and pain, cough medicines if the cough is causing fatigue, pain, or sleep loss. Fluids—as tolerated—should be encouraged, to clear toxins through the kidneys. Isolate your child from the rest of the family. To minimize the probability of contracting other diseases he should not return to school during convalescence.

PRECAUTIONS

● Watch for signs of complications and report their occurrence to your doctor. ● Without complications, the fever associated with influenza often peaks in two cycles (diphasic). It is elevated for a day or two, normal for a day, and elevated for a day or two. Do not misinterpret 24 hours of normal temperature as a "cure," and do not allow your child to resume activities until his temperature is normal for two or more days and he is feeling well.

continued

DOCTOR'S TREATMENT

Your doctor's treatment is the same as home treatment. Antibiotics, cultures, blood count, and possibly hospitalization may be required to treat complications.

Preventative vaccines have limited usefulness in children. Influenza viruses frequently mutate (spontaneously change their structure) from year to year, and last year's vaccine may be useless against this year's virus. Moreover, reactions to influenza vaccines in children are frequent, though rarely serious. The current thinking is that only children at special risk from influenza should have annual immunization. The conditions that constitute special risks are: rheumatic heart disease, congenital and hypertensive heart disease, cystic fibrosis, severe asthma, tuberculosis, nephrosis, chronic nephritis, chronic disease of the nervous system, and diabetes.

The prescription for flu is bed rest, acetaminophen, and isolation.

Ingrown Toenails

DESCRIPTION

The corners and edges of toenails may break the skin surrounding the nail. Once the skin is broken, conditions exist that encourage infection. The infection causes the tissues to swell, further embedding the corner of the nail. The toe becomes red, painful, and tender to the touch, and thin, watery pus is discharged from the wound and works its way under the nail. This condition is known as ingrown toenail, and no healing is possible as long as the nail remains within the wound.

The initial wound may be caused by injury to the toe as a result of being stepped on or squeezed by ill-fitting shoes. Or the nail may have been trimmed in a manner that creates a sharp spur at the corner that pierces the skin like a dagger as the nail grows.

Most cases of ingrown toenails involve the big toes of older children but any toe can be involved. A baby can develop an ingrown toenail by digging his bare toes into the mat of the crib or other surface where he has been placed face down.

DIAGNOSIS

There should be no difficulty recognizing the gradually worsening tenderness, redness, pain, and swelling that eventually involve one entire side of a toenail. Often the nail becomes partly covered by raw, red tissue (granulation tissue) and a wet crust.

HOME TREATMENT

Recognized early, an ingrown toenail can be successfully treated by gently cutting out the spur or the ingrown corner of the nail and then soaking the toe for a long time. Even if the embedded nail cannot be removed because of the tenderness, proper and prolonged soaking in a strong Epsom salts solution (one cup to one quart of water) may cure the condition. Because of the delicacy of the nails involved, the ingrown toenails of infants can often be cured by wiping them several times a day with rubbing alcohol.

PRECAUTIONS

● If your child repeatedly develops ingrown toenails, check for shoes that are too small or too pointed. ● Check your child's method of trimming his toenails.

DOCTOR'S TREATMENT

Your doctor's treatment will often be the same as home treatment, although your doctor is able to use a local anesthetic to remove the embedded nail and do a more thorough job. If ingrown toenails frequently occur, your doctor may suggest minor surgery that permanently narrows the nail and makes ingrowing less likely.

Insect Bites

DESCRIPTION

The bites and stings of most insects are minor annoyances to most children. The only common complication is impetigo from scratching. Some insect bites can cause serious illnesses:

Black widow spiders can inject a venom potent enough to kill.

The *brown recluse spider* bite can cause a large sloughing ulcer and fever.

Female wood tick bites can cause an ascending paralysis and death.

Bees, wasps, hornets, and yellow jackets can cause severe reactions (anaphylaxis) in persons who are allergic—generalized hives, asthma, circulatory collapse, and death.

Some children become sensitized (allergic) to the bites of mosquitoes, stable flies, fleas, and lice, but the allergic reactions are usually less severe than those caused by stinging insects.

Among diseases transmitted by insect bites are Rocky Mountain spotted fever, Colorado tick fever, and tularemia (wood ticks), rickettsialpox (mouse mites), viral encephalitis (mosquitoes), and typhus (red mites, lice, and rat fleas).

DIAGNOSIS

Flying insects usually bite only exposed areas of the skin. Crawling insects bite anywhere and often in groups. Flea bites tend to be concentrated on the ankles and lower legs. Bedbug bites often appear as three to five bites arranged in a relatively straight line, an inch or two apart. Honeybees leave the stinger in the bite; bumblebees and other stinging insects do not. Ticks remain attached to the skin for long periods while biting, and resemble small, plump raisins.

HOME TREATMENT

In most instances insect bites can be treated by applying cold for a few minutes followed by an application of calamine lotion. Oral antihistamines reduce the itching and minimize the swelling. Biting ticks should be grasped as close to the skin as possible with tweezers and removed, making sure the head is not left in the wound.

PRECAUTIONS

● Protect children with proper clothing, mosquito-netting, and insect repellents. ● Learn to recognize the insects in your locale and to know their characteristics. ● If your child is bitten by a black widow spider (or if the sting is from a bee, wasp, or the like) and the child develops hives, or if breathing, speaking, or swallowing is difficult, contact your doctor or local emergency room immediately.

DOCTOR'S TREATMENT

Allergic reactions are treated with epinephrine, antihistamines, or steroids. A child who is allergic should have desensitizing injections. Also, your doctor may prescribe a kit for immediate home treatment.

Your doctor will give antivenom for use against black widow spider bites.

Protect your child with mosquito netting and insect repellents.

Intestinal Allergies

DESCRIPTION

Infants are the most likely sufferers of intestinal allergies. The condition involves vomiting, diarrhea, and abdominal cramps and occurs from minutes to hours after the child has ingested certain foods, beverages, or medications. The most common offending food is nonpasteurized cow's milk; but eggs, wheat, soybean formulas, orange juice, tomatoes, chocolate, fish, berries, and melons may also be responsible. Sometimes, blood may be seen in the stools; other signs include hives, eczema, runny nose, and asthma.

Resembling the symptoms of an intestinal allergy but in fact not allergies at all are the malabsorption syndromes, which result in "failure to thrive." A malabsorption syndrome arises from an enzyme deficiency. Normally, the intestines and the pancreas produce enzymes that break down starches, fats, proteins, and sugars. In a malabsorption syndrome, an enzyme is missing, and certain foods cannot be digested.

DIAGNOSIS

If a particular food brings on abdominal cramps and diarrhea (with or without vomiting), an intestinal allergy or malabsorption syndrome can be suspected. By judiciously changing the child's diet and observing the child's physical reactions, you may make a preliminary diagnosis. Often, however, specific and complex tests are required.

HOME TREATMENT

If your infant begins to vomit or has cramps or diarrhea after a new food has been introduced into his diet, stop the food promptly. Add new foods one at a time and allow several days between introductions.

PRECAUTIONS

• Persistent diarrhea is a clue to a malabsorption or an allergy problem. Broad-spectrum antibiotics and gastrointestinal viruses may cause a temporary loss of digestive enzymes, particularly lactase (the enzyme that digests milk sugar). Temporarily eliminate milk and milk products if diarrhea persists. • Symptoms of malabsorption call for a sweat test to rule out cystic fibrosis.

DOCTOR'S TREATMENT

Doctors diagnose these maladies on the basis of: dietary changes; culture and examination of stools for blood, fat, and starch; analysis of digestive enzymes; biopsy of the intestinal lining; sugar (lactose, glucose, and xylose) tolerance tests; sweat test; chest X rays; and other factors. Treatment involves dietary control and, sometimes, a prescription of digestive enzyme supplements.

Jaundice in Children

DESCRIPTION
Jaundice is a yellowing of the skin and the whites of the eyes due to the accumulation of bilirubin in the body. When a child has jaundice, all of the body fluids are stained; the tears are yellow, and the urine is dark orange.

Bilirubin comes from the hemoglobin that is released when old red blood cells are replaced by new cells. It is excreted by the liver into the intestine as bile. Jaundice develops when the red blood cells are rapidly destroyed (as in sickle cell, Mediterranean, spherocytic, and other, rarer forms of anemia); when the liver cannot transform bilirubin into bile; or when bile cannot flow through the bile ducts into the intestines. Certain medications may temporarily impede the function of the liver and bring on jaundice. Blockage of the bile ducts by stones, cysts, or congenital malformation can also provoke jaundice. The disease may be caused by some drugs and poisons and is rarely the complication of more generalized infection.

The usual cause of jaundice in children over one month of age is hepatitis. Damage to the liver cells by the hepatitis virus interferes with the formation of bile.

DIAGNOSIS
The yellow-gold-orange color of the skin and whites of the eyes suggests jaundice. However, the diagnosis can be exceedingly complex and depends upon laboratory tests.

HOME TREATMENT
Only after a clear diagnosis has been made can anything be done in the home. Then, antihistamines may lessen the itching of jaundice.

PRECAUTIONS
None.

DOCTOR'S TREATMENT
Doctors usually hospitalize children with suspected jaundice to treat the problem and to conduct laboratory tests.

Jaundice in Newborns

DESCRIPTION

Because a newborn infant's nervous system is vulnerable to permanent damage, jaundice during the first days of life has special significance. Jaundice occurs in infants due to an excessive breakdown of red blood cells or to the liver's inability to rapidly remove bilirubin from the blood.

Sixty percent of full-term infants and eighty percent of premature babies develop jaundice during the first week of life. This occurs due to the rapid destruction of the excess number of red blood cells with which all healthy babies are born. It usually begins on the second or third day of life and disappears between the fifth and tenth day.

The two most frequent causes of abnormal jaundice in the newborn are erythroblastosis fetalis and sepsis (blood poisoning). Erythroblastosis fetalis is due to an incompatibility between the blood of the child and the mother. Because of the incompatibility, the mother forms antibodies that rapidly destroy the infant's red blood cells. Sepsis (a generalized infection caused by bacteria or viruses) causes jaundice in the newborn by destroying red blood cells and injuring the liver.

Breast-fed newborns may also develop jaundice because a substance in the mother's milk interferes with the function of the liver.

There are scores of other causes of jaundice in the newborn, including congenital anemias (Cooley's, spherocytic, sickle cell), hepatitis, and German measles, but they are rare.

DIAGNOSIS

Because erythroblastosis fetalis and sepsis can be fatal to newborn babies if not treated immediately, a doctor's diagnosis must be made promptly. Other forms of jaundice can also be serious if the bilirubin in the blood exceeds a safe level. In suspected cases of jaundice, a doctor must monitor the bilirubin level closely.

HOME TREATMENT

Parents, it is your responsibility to watch out for the development of jaundice in the first week of your child's life at home. To judge the yellowness of the skin and eyes accurately, observe the baby in natural light. (Artificial light obscures the true color.)

PRECAUTIONS

● Jaundice in the first 24 hours of life is abnormal. ● Jaundice that develops or worsens after a baby leaves the hospital should be reported to your doctor. ● Poor nursing, excessive drowsiness, irritability, and fever in a jaundiced baby should be reported immediately. ● If your infant develops jaundice follow your physician's directions to the letter.

DOCTOR'S TREATMENT

Blood tests and cultures define the cause of the jaundice and its progress. To lower the bilirubin level your doctor may expose the baby to ultraviolet light or replace the infant's blood with that of a donor.

Laryngitis

DESCRIPTION

Laryngitis is an inflammation of the voice box (larynx). It is closely related to croup; but unlike croup, it isn't associated with breathing difficulties. Laryngitis is almost always due to a respiratory virus. Symptoms are hoarseness, dry hacking cough, scratchy throat, low-grade (101°F) or no fever. Laryngitis may last from one to fourteen days.

DIAGNOSIS

Diagnosis is based on the typical symptoms of hoarseness and dry cough without any breathing difficulty.

HOME TREATMENT

Plug in a vaporizer. Give your child warm drinks, and place warm compresses on his neck. Hush him gently if he tries to speak. Give him acetaminophen for fever or pain and an expectorant cough remedy for temporary relief of cough.

PRECAUTIONS

● If any breathing difficulty arises, notify a doctor. ● If a child has a climbing fever, difficulty breathing, and a cough, he may have an inflammation of the epiglottis (the structure in the back of the throat that prevents food from entering the larynx and windpipe). ● Inflammation of the epiglottis is a medical emergency; **take your child to a doctor immediately.**

DOCTOR'S TREATMENT

Doctors will verify the diagnosis and rule out other conditions during the physical examination. They may take a throat culture and a complete blood count. If laryngitis is prolonged, your doctor may x-ray your child's chest and neck or refer you to an ear, nose, and throat specialist.

Lazy Eye

DESCRIPTION

A "lazy eye" is one in which the vision is poor because the image received by that eye is suppressed (amblyopia ex anopsia—loss of vision from disuse). Most cases result from weakness of one or more of the six small muscles that move the eyeball. The condition also can result from marked near- or farsightedness, astigmatism, or other interference with vision in one eye (congenital cataracts, scars on the cornea, etc.).

Eye muscle weaknesses can cause the eyes to turn in or out in relation to each other. This can lead to the child's seeing double. If a young child learns to ignore one of the double images, a loss of vision in that eye results. On the other hand, if the eye muscles are normal, but the vision is poor in one eye, the young child may ignore the poor image received.

DIAGNOSIS

Lazy eye should be suspected when the eyes are not parallel all or most of the time or are parallel less and less often in a child under seven years of age. Your doctor will inspect the insides and outsides of both eyes and test their movements in all directions. Vision will be checked with a letter or picture chart when your child is old enough to understand directions. A younger child's vision should be checked by an ophthalmologist using an indirect method.

HOME TREATMENT

No home treatment is advised until a doctor has diagnosed the condition.

PRECAUTIONS

The only precaution is catching the condition in time to correct it. See your doctor if: ● your child's eyes aren't parallel; ● the pupil of one is a different color than the other; ● your child (past the age of two) has trouble seeing or judging distances when reaching for an object; or ● your child cocks his head to one side or turns his face to see better (he may be compensating for double vision). ● Have your child's vision checked each year after age three or four. Amblyopia can be treated successfully in children up to age seven. If untreated the condition may become permanent.

DOCTOR'S TREATMENT

Amblyopia is corrected by an operation, by patching the good eye, or by hindering the vision in the good eye with eye drops or glasses.

Leukemia

DESCRIPTION

Leukemia is cancer of the white blood cells. It can afflict children at any age, but it most frequently occurs in children between three and four years old. The disease may progress slowly or rapidly. A quarter of the cases are detected during routine physical exams before the child has any symptoms.

Typical symptoms of leukemia are: anemia (indicated by paleness, weakness, or tiredness); spontaneous bruises on the body; swollen, red, and bleeding gums; low-grade fever (101°F); a visible swelling of some lymph nodes (not tender and not red); bone pain; uncontrollable and frequently recurrent nosebleeds; and blood in the urine or stools.

DIAGNOSIS

Doctors may suspect the disease when a physical exam reveals the above signs and symptoms and an enlarged spleen or liver. Suspicion is strengthened by an abnormal blood count that shows malignant white blood cells. The diagnosis is confirmed by an examination of bone marrow.

HOME TREATMENT

None.

PRECAUTIONS

Although it is rare, leukemia is one of the four "common" forms of cancer in children. Many illnesses imitate leukemia, and they are NOT rare; for example, infectious mononucleosis, herpes infections of the mouth, vitamin C deficiency, rheumatic fever, rheumatoid arthritis, sickle cell anemia, and other diseases that cause spontaneous bruising. Do not jump to the conclusion that your child has leukemia because of the presence of any of the above signs or symptoms. See your doctor to ease your mind.

DOCTOR'S TREATMENT

Today, leukemia can be treated with a wide range of anticancer drugs. These drugs may result in long periods of remission and even cure. Pediatric oncologists (cancer specialists) choose and supervise the treatment of leukemia.

Measles

DESCRIPTION

Also known as *rubeola,* measles is a highly contagious illness caused by a specific virus. It is characterized by high fever, severe cough, and rash, and frequently sparks severe complications. Measles passes from child to child by an airborne or droplet-borne virus; it has an incubation period of ten to twelve days. The disease can be passed on to others any time between the fifth day of incubation through the first few days of the rash.

Measles' first symptoms are a runny nose, reddish eyes, cough, and fever. After three or four days the fever rises to 104°F or 105°F, the cough worsens and a heavy, splotchy, red rash begins on the neck and face. The rash quickly spreads over the trunk, arms, and legs. When the rash has erupted fully, the fever breaks, and the child improves if no complications set in.

Common complications of a bout with measles include viral and bacterial pneumonias and middle ear infections. Encephalitis (inflammation of the brain) occurs in one or two of every 1,000 cases.

Measles in children who have received only the dead virus vaccine produces a high fever, prostration, and a rash of blisters and petechiae (purplish-red spots). It often is complicated by pneumonia.

DIAGNOSIS

The diagnosis cannot be made during early stages of the disease. Just before the rash develops, spots that look like grains of salt surrounded by a red rim (Koplik's spots) appear inside the cheeks near the molars.

HOME TREATMENT

Give your child acetaminophen to reduce the fever and a cough suppressant to ease a severe cough. Keep him away from bright light; light bothers but does not injure the eyes. Have your child drink extra liquids if he can, and give him antiemetics if he is vomiting.

PRECAUTIONS

● If the fever and cough do not subside as the rash peaks, suspect complications. Watch for earaches, which signify middle ear infection. ● A newborn baby is immune to measles for three to six months only if his mother is immune. ● Be sure your child receives the proper, lifelong immunization against measles.

DOCTOR'S TREATMENT

If your child has not been immunized and has been exposed to the virus, your doctor can give injections of gamma globulin within six or seven days of exposure to prevent or modify the disease.

Meningitis

DESCRIPTION

Meningitis is an infection of the meninges, the layers of tissue that cover and protect the brain and spinal cord. Most often, meningitis is caused by bacterial infection. Usually contracted by direct contact with, or airborne droplets from, a healthy *carrier*, meningitis seldom is spread by a person with the disease. Its incubation period is one to seven days.

Meningitis may be a complication of a skull fracture if the fracture has extended into the nose, middle ear, or nasal sinus. Sometimes, meningitis follows an upper respiratory tract infection or middle ear infection. Its characteristic symptoms are moderate to high fever, headache, vomiting, prostration, convulsions, and a stiff neck—the child cannot touch his chin to his chest with his mouth closed. The tripod sign in which the child sits with his arms braced behind him for support is typical. (Purplish red spots called petechiae scattered over the body, together with fever, indicate a probable meningococcus infection.)

DIAGNOSIS

The diagnosis can only be made with certainty by testing spinal fluid obtained by a spinal tap.

HOME TREATMENT

Meningitis is a medical emergency in which hours, if not minutes, count. **Do not attempt any home treatment.**

PRECAUTIONS

● The unnecessary use of antibiotics for an upper respiratory tract infection may mask the onset of meningitis. A child who is prostrated with fever and a stiff neck and has petechiae on the body is in danger and should be taken to a medical facility immediately.

DOCTOR'S TREATMENT

Your doctor will take a complete history and perform a physical and neurologic exam, followed by a spinal tap. Spinal fluid will be examined for cells, bacteria, and abnormal chemical components. (This is the only way to differentiate between meningitis and encephalitis, which is also a life-threatening disease.) A culture of the spinal fluid, blood, nose and throat mucus, and petechiae may also be done. Immediately following the spinal tap and cultures your doctor will administer intravenous fluids and antibiotics.

Motion Sickness

DESCRIPTION
Car-, air-, and seasickness are all forms of motion sickness. Sufficient rhythmic motion up and down or side to side will make most children nauseated, presumably because of the effect on the balance mechanism of the inner ears. Some children are more susceptible than others; young infants are apparently immune.

A motion-sick child becomes nauseated, pale or "green," and anxious; he may perspire and vomit. Motion sickness is not self-induced nor can the victim control it. It can be serious.

DIAGNOSIS
Motion sickness is fairly obvious. Susceptible children will have recurrent attacks.

HOME TREATMENT
Consult your doctor about antinauseants. Give your child an antinauseant by mouth one hour before the start of each trip and every four hours during the trip. Dimenhydrinate antinauseant tablets or liquid is highly effective and safe. Lying down with eyes closed, coolness, preoccupation with a game, and a light diet will minimize motion sickness.

PRECAUTIONS
● Prolonged motion sickness (over hours) can eventually result in excessive vomiting, vomiting of blood, and dehydration.

DOCTOR'S TREATMENT
Your doctor's treatment will be the same as your home treatment unless your child's symptoms have progressed to dehydration and gastric bleeding, which require hospitalization and intravenous fluids.

Mumps

DESCRIPTION

Mumps is a moderately contagious infection by a specific virus, which involves the salivary glands. It is contracted by contact with saliva from a person with mumps. The incubation period for mumps is 14 to 21 days. The disease can be passed on any time from two or more days before symptoms appear until all symptoms have disappeared. One attack confers lifelong immunity; if attacks seem to recur, they are due to other diseases of the salivary gland.

Typical symptoms include fever (low-grade 101°F or as high as 105°F), loss of appetite, and headache. One or two days after onset of these symptoms, one or more salivary glands become painfully swollen; swelling lasts about a week.

Complications of mumps include encephalitis and permanent deafness. The disease may even involve the ovaries and testicles or cause an infection of the pancreas.

DIAGNOSIS

The diagnosis of a typical case of the mumps is obvious from the swelling of the parotid salivary gland that lies behind, below, and in front of the earlobe. Only a swelling of the parotid gland has the earlobe as its center. Other salivary glands, such as the submaxillary salivary glands, which lie under the edge of the jaw, may be swollen with or without involvement of the parotids, and swelling may occur on one or both sides of the face.

Problems of diagnosis arise when complications of mumps develop before, or sometimes even without, swelling of the salivary glands. Then, the cause of abdominal pain (involvement of the pancreas or ovaries), the swollen, tender testicles, or the signs of encephalitis may be difficult to link with mumps.

HOME TREATMENT

Moderate rest and isolation are recommended until all symptoms are gone. Acetaminophen may be given to reduce pain and fever. Avoid feeding the child spicy foods.

PRECAUTIONS

● Infants from four to six months of age are immune only if their mothers are immune. ● Routine immunization against mumps is strongly advised. ● Attacks that seem to recur are not due to mumps but to inflammation of the parotid salivary gland (often allergic in nature), a stone in the salivary duct, or a bacterial infection of the gland. They should be reported to your doctor.

DOCTOR'S TREATMENT

If complications are present, your doctor may have to order a spinal tap or blood tests to measure the number of mumps antibodies in the blood. Doctors do not follow any specific treatment, but may hospitalize a child to arrive at a diagnosis or to provide supportive treatment. A child may receive mumps vaccine shortly after exposure to the disease.

Nosebleeds

DESCRIPTION

Nosebleeds are as much a part of normal childhood as scraped knees and bruised shins. Ninety-nine percent of them arise from the rupture of tiny blood vessels in the septum (midline partition of the nose) located about one-quarter inch in from the nostrils. These small arteries, veins, and capillaries are easily broken by a minor blow to the nose. A scab forms during healing and is easily disturbed by rubbing or picking, which reactivates the bleeding. This sequence of events may be further aggravated by: allergies or a head cold that dilates the blood vessels in the nose; heated air that dries out the nasal membranes; sneezing, coughing, and blowing the nose; and by a child rubbing and scratching his nose, especially during sleep (most nosebleeds start at night).

DIAGNOSIS

A nosebleed is fairly obvious. Since the two sides of the nose join in the back and with the throat and the esophagus (which lead to the stomach), blood may flow from both nostrils and from the mouth, and may be vomited.

HOME TREATMENT

Your child should be taught at an early age how to stop a nosebleed by himself. He should be instructed to remain calm and to sit upright with his head held high to decrease blood pressure. He should grasp the whole lower half of his nose between his thumb and fingers and compress both sides in this way firmly against the septum. The nose should be held for ten minutes to allow the blood to clot. If bleeding recurs when the pressure is released, a large clot in the nose is probably preventing the broken blood vessel from retracting. Have your child blow his nose vigorously to dislodge the clot. After the clot has been removed, repeat compression of the nose for ten to twelve minutes.

To prevent recurring nosebleeds, put ointment (petroleum jelly or antibiotic ointment) up the nose in the morning and evening for seven to fourteen days. Add moisture to the night air with a vaporizer or humidifier. Give the child antihistamines if he has an allergy, or oral decongestants if he has a head cold.

PRECAUTIONS

● Do not merely pinch nostrils together; compress the entire soft portion of the nose. Otherwise, the blood simply will dam up and run down the throat. ● Do not lay your child down. ● Remain calm and reassure your child. ● Cold compresses, pressure on the upper lip, nose drops, and other household remedies are unnecessary. ● Do not pack the nose with cotton or gauze.

DOCTOR'S TREATMENT

Generally, your doctor's treatment will be the same as your home treatment and is necessary only when you are unable to follow the above directions. If the nosebleed is due to an allergy or a cold, your doctor will treat those conditions.

Pigeon Toes

DESCRIPTION

Toeing-in of the feet, particularly when standing and walking, is known as pigeon toes. After birth, the position and shape of the feet and legs reflect the position they held during the last weeks *in utero*. By the age of three months, the child's feet and legs should have assumed a normal shape.

Throughout infancy and early childhood, the position of the feet and legs can be influenced by the manner in which they are held while the child is lying down and sitting. If the child habitually sleeps face down with his toes directed inward, pigeon toes development is encouraged. Sitting on the haunches with the knees sharply flexed and the toes directed outward also may lead to pigeon toes.

Pigeon toes also may result from a deformity of the foot, the lower leg, or the thigh. Depending on the severity of the deformity, the child's toes will point inward to a great or small degree. A child who has a marked deformity will tend to trip over his feet until he learns to compensate for the handicap.

DIAGNOSIS

If you suspect deformity of your child's feet or legs, consult your doctor.

HOME TREATMENT

By three months of age, your infant will prefer to sleep with his toes directed outward. This position is normal and should be encouraged. When your child is old enough to sit upright, his feet should be straight or turned outward. And until 18 to 24 months, you toddler usually will walk with one or both feet turned outward for a wider base and better balance. This, too, is normal. A tendency to toe in after three months of age should be called to your doctor's attention.

PRECAUTIONS

● An uncorrected foot deformity makes proper shoe-fitting difficult and eventually may lead to a skewed foot with bunions in adolescence or adulthood. A child who sits on the floor should be taught to sit cross-legged, not on his haunches. ● Corrective orthopedic shoes should be prescribed only by a medical professional, not by a shoe salesman. ● Most minor cases of pigeon toes correct themselves. Nevertheless, let a doctor help you judge whether the condition is minor or not.

DOCTOR'S TREATMENT

Your doctor will observe your child while he stands and walks with and without shoes. The feet, lower and upper legs, and the rotation of the hips will be examined. If a case of pigeon toes is mild, nothing need be done. To correct a foot deformity after three months of age, your doctor will order specific kinds of shoes or plaster casts. To correct a deformity of the lower leg, a splint that holds the feet outwardly rotated while the child sleeps will be prescribed. Your doctor will probably not treat a deformity of the thigh until your child is an adolescent. If the condition has not corrected itself by that time, surgery may be necessary.

Pinworms

DESCRIPTION

The pinworm, a distant cousin of the earthworm, lives only in humans and the higher apes. The adult pinworm is one-quarter to one-half inch in length, white in color, and about as thick as stout sewing thread. It lives in the large intestine and, moving with a caterpillar-like motion, comes out at night to lay its microscopic-size eggs on the skin around the anus. The eggs are transmitted from the skin to the mouth by the hands or via toys and food and are swallowed. The eggs hatch, and two to six weeks later the larvae have developed into mature, egg-laying adult pinworms and the cycle continues. (Pinworms may be transmitted to other children and to adults in the same manner described above.)

A child with pinworms will have few symptoms. He may complain at night of itching or burning around the anal or genital area. If the infestation is heavy he may have abdominal cramps. Pinworms may cause appendicitis (though rarely), and they may work their way into a girl's vagina and urethra causing vaginitis and cystitis to develop.

DIAGNOSIS

Usually the diagnosis is easily made by examining the skin around the anus at night while the child sleeps or just after he has awakened. Pinworms head back into the anus if disturbed by light; so the search must be done quickly. A pinworm can be mistaken for lint on the skin; if the lint moves, it is a pinworm. Occasionally, pinworms may be found in a bowel movement.

HOME TREATMENT

Vermifuges (worm medicines) must be obtained by prescription, but many doctors will prescribe them over the telephone. The course of treatment with any of these drugs may be repeated once or twice if you allow seven to ten days between each series. When one member of a family has pinworms, all members (except infants) should receive treatment.

PRECAUTIONS

● Suspect that pinworms may be the cause of recurrent cystitis or vaginitis. ● If one member of a family has pinworms, launder his underclothes, bed linens, and towels to destroy the worms' eggs. Also, cut and scrub his fingernails to remove any eggs. ● Do not mistake lint or thread for pinworms; look for movement. ● Do not blame household cats and dogs for pinworms. These worms live only in humans.

DOCTOR'S TREATMENT

Your doctor will investigate for pinworms using a National Institutes of Health swab or tape with which eggs from the skin can be picked up. A microscopic examination will be made of the swab or tape. The doctor's treatment will be the same as your home treatment.

Pneumonia

DESCRIPTION

Pneumonia is an infection of one or more areas of the lungs that is caused by bacteria or viruses.

Bacterial pneumonia. To contract bacterial pneumonia requires the simultaneous presence of a causative germ and a receptive host. Causative bacteria frequently are present in the nose and throat of healthy children. Before these organisms can invade the lungs, however, your child's resistance must be lowered by a cold or some other upper respiratory tract infection. So bacterial pneumonia is not considered to be contagious in the usual sense.

The symptoms of bacterial pneumonia include a mild upper respiratory tract infection, followed by the sudden onset of high fever (105°F), chills, cough, rapid breathing, and sometimes pain on either or both sides of the chest. In infants the respiratory distress may cause flaring of the nostrils, retractions of the soft spaces of the chest, and grunting sounds on exhalation.

Viral pneumonia. These so-called walking pneumonias are contagious. The incubation period for most viruses is two to five days. The onset of viral pneumonia is gradual, creating symptoms of headache, fatigue, fever of variable (100°F-105°F) degree, a sore throat, and a severe, dry cough.

DIAGNOSIS

The diagnosis requires careful examination of the chest, X rays, a complete blood count, and cultures of the blood and the sputum.

HOME TREATMENT

Many cases of viral pneumonia that are mild and unrecognized and treated with cold remedies subside spontaneously after 10 to 14 days.

PRECAUTIONS

● Sudden worsening of a cold coupled with high fever, cough, chills, chest pain, or rapid breathing suggests pneumonia. ● In infants, flaring of the nostrils, retractions of the chest, and grunting breathing are serious symptoms and warrant immediate medical care. ● In children, sputum tinged with blood may or may not be serious, but it indicates the need for a doctor's attention.

DOCTOR'S TREATMENT

Your doctor will diagnose pneumonia by means of the physical examination and laboratory tests. In the past a child with pneumonia was always hospitalized. Now, only the youngest and the most severely ill are hospitalized.

Most pneumonias respond to antibiotics, but viral pneumonias do not.

Poisoning

DESCRIPTION

In the United States the usual cause of poisoning among children between the ages of one and five years is an overdose of aspirin. Then come soaps, detergents, cleansers, bleaches, vitamins, iron tonics, insecticides, plants, polishes and waxes, hormones, and tranquilizers. Less common but more toxic poisons include boric acid, oil of wintergreen, volatile hydrocarbons (gasoline, kerosene, turpentine, naphtha, cleaning fluids), strong acids, alkalis (drain and oven cleaners), and many prescription and over-the-counter medications (including aspirin substitutes and acetaminophen).

DIAGNOSIS

The diagnosis of poisoning depends primarily upon an accurate history. Without one, the diagnosis relies on suspicion, a careful physical examination for telltale clues, and laboratory tests. Usually, the telltale signs of aspirin overdose are an increased rate of breathing, ringing in the ears, nausea, excitation, and coma. Poisoning from acids and alkalis causes burns on the lips, mouth, and tongue. An overdose of an iron tonic produces abdominal pain and severe, often bloody vomiting, followed by collapse.

HOME TREATMENT

Two steps are vital. First, try to determine quickly how much of the substance your child has taken and when. Second, call your doctor or a local poison control center for instructions. Read the label of the drug or other preparation over the phone. You will be advised whether or not to induce vomiting.

If your child has not vomited, if the poison was neither a strong acid nor an alkali, and if your child is conscious, induce vomiting by giving two to three teaspoonful of syrup of ipecac followed by a half to a full glass of water or juice. (**Do not give milk.**) If vomiting does not occur within 20 to 30 minutes, repeat the syrup of ipecac liquid dose. To induce vomiting may not be safe after volatile hydrocarbons have been swallowed.

PRECAUTIONS

● The most important precaution is to see that all poisonous substances are stored out of reach of children—under lock and key if necessary. ● Do not place or store dangerous substances in anything other than their original containers (for example, kerosene left in a drinking glass, medication kept in an unlabeled container). ● Insist upon child-proof tops on all medicines, not just those for children. ● More children are fatally poisoned by adult aspirin than by children's flavored aspirin. ● Be careful with iron tablets. They taste sweet, look like candy, and can be deadly. ● When visiting others' homes, do not let your children explore until you are sure there are no poisons within reach. ● Keep the telephone numbers of the police and fire departments, your doctor, and the local poison control center near the telephone. ● Always have syrup of ipecac in the house.

DOCTOR'S TREATMENT

Treatment depends upon an accurate history and a thoughtful diagnosis. Only a few specific antidotes are available to reverse poisoning from among thousands of poisonous substances. Your doctor may induce vomiting with syrup of ipecac or wash out the stomach by means of a tube. Further treatment varies with the substance ingested and your child's condition.

Make sure that all poisonous substances are locked away, out of reach of children.

Poison Ivy

DESCRIPTION

Rashes among children in the two- to twelve-year-old age group are generally due to contact with certain agents, the most common of which is vine poison ivy. (Other weeds, such as poison oak and poison sumac, and toys, cosmetics, and chemicals used in the manufacture of clothing and shoes are also responsible.)

Poison ivy rash develops in sensitive children after direct contact with any part of the vine. It also may occur after exposure to smoke from the burning vine or from the coats of pets that have touched the plant. Poison ivy rash can be spread to any part of the skin by the hands, fingernails, and contaminated clothing.

Itching develops within two to 24 hours after contact with poison ivy. It is followed by a reddening and swelling (edema) of the skin. Pin-sized, clear blisters develop and may merge to create blisters as large as one-half inch. The rash often appears in straight lines where the plant has brushed against the skin or where the child has scratched. Poison ivy is often carried to a boy's penis by his hands.

DIAGNOSIS

A blistered, itching rash that appears in straight lines is indicative of poison ivy. However, the rash may appear generally over the skin and look similar to other rashes.

HOME TREATMENT

Promptly bathing the child with soap and water and cutting and scrubbing the fingernails will remove much of the poison ivy from the skin. Laundering removes it from contaminated clothing.

The most effective treatment of a small rash is to rub in a steroid ointment three or four times a day. Large rashes are best treated by oral steroids for four to five days. Check with your doctor. Calamine lotion and oral antihistamines lessen the itching.

PRECAUTIONS

● If poison ivy continues to spread after four to seven days, your child is still coming into contact with the plant, directly or indirectly. Try to find the source. ● Scratching can result in impetigo; so watch for signs of infection. ● Teach your child to recognize the vine. ● Make sure your child is dressed appropriately (in long pants and socks) when in the woods and around campsites.

DOCTOR'S TREATMENT

Your doctor will confirm the diagnosis, treat any secondary infection, and prescribe steroids as needed. Vaccines designed to desensitize people against poison ivy are available, but they are not always effective. Oral preparations are even less helpful.

Polio

DESCRIPTION
Also known as *poliomyelitis* and *infantile paralysis,* polio is an infection of the central nervous system that is due to three related but different viruses. An attack by one type of virus confers lifelong immunity against that type only. Therefore, it is possible to have three separate attacks of the disease.

Polio virus is found in the saliva and the stools of patients, and it is transmitted by direct contact or fecal contamination through swimming pools, toys, or food. The incubation period for polio is three to fourteen days.

Of those children who develop polio, 93 to 95 percent of them have no symptoms but develop immunity. Four to five percent of those infected develop a minor illness, with fever, malaise, sore throat, and nausea for three to four days. One to two percent develop clinically recognizable polio, with symptoms of a minor illness plus sore, stiff muscles and a stiff neck and spine. Within this one or two percent are the children who become paralyzed or die.

DIAGNOSIS
Minor illness cases may never be recognized as polio, unless they occur as part of an epidemic. Diagnosis is based on examination of viral cultures and studies of antibodies in the blood. Central nervous system involvement is suspected when an ill child has a stiff neck and back and must support himself tripod-fashion (when sitting on the floor, the child must brace himself with both arms; hence, tripod). It is confirmed by the results of a spinal tap, cultures, or antibody studies.

HOME TREATMENT
The imperative home treatment is prevention through immunization. Oral, live virus vaccine (Sabin) is effective against all three types of polio, and it confers long-lasting immunity.

PRECAUTIONS
● Infants are temporarily immune to each of the three types of polio for four to six months only if their mothers are immune. A full series of oral vaccine is needed to achieve long-lasting immunity. ● Anyone who has received injections of original, dead vaccine (Salk) must have boosters or two full series of the oral vaccine to guarantee immunity. ● Polio virus still exists in this country and in many other countries of the world. Avoidance isn't possible; immunity is essential.

DOCTOR'S TREATMENT
Your doctor's diagnosis will be made on the basis of a physical examination and the results of a spinal tap. A child with a suspected or known case of polio will be isolated. A child who is not immunized and has been exposed to the disease will be given gamma globulin. A child who has contracted polio will be given aspirin, acetaminophen, codeine, opiates, and hot packs to reduce the pain. If he is paralyzed by the disease, an artificial respirator, a tracheostomy, prolonged physical therapy, braces or orthopedic surgery may be required.

Puncture Wounds

DESCRIPTION

Wounds that pierce the skin are classified as abrasions (scrapes), lacerations (cuts), and punctures. A puncture is a wound whose depth is greater than its length and width. Most puncture wounds in children are made by nails, needles, pins, knives, and splinters.

Because of their small opening and their depth, punctures have four particular dangers: the tetanus germ thrives in the absence of air, so punctures are ideal sites for developing tetanus; they are hard to clean, so punctures are susceptible to infection; punctures can penetrate deep into the body; and they may harbor foreign bodies that are difficult to detect.

DIAGNOSIS

The presence of a puncture wound usually is obvious. The important aspects of the diagnosis involve determining whether the puncture has penetrated into a deeper structure (joint, abdominal or thoracic cavity, skull, or tendon), whether it contains a foreign body (broken needle, wood or glass splinter, or shred of clothing), and whether it is infected.

HOME TREATMENT

Wash the skin surrounding the puncture with soap and water and apply a nonirritating (nonstinging, nonburning, noninjurious) antiseptic, such as solution—not tincture—of Merthiolate antiseptic. Be sure your child's tetanus immunization is up to date (within five years). Make sure that the instrument that made the wound is intact and has not broken off at the tip. Inspect and feel the wound to determine if a foreign body can be detected under the skin. Cover the wound with a sterile bandage and inspect it twice a day for signs of infection (redness, discharge, swelling, increasing pain, and tenderness).

PRECAUTIONS

● Puncture wounds in the abdomen or chest may be very serious. Be sure to take your child to a doctor. ● Punctures of a joint may cause purulent arthritis within hours. The knee joint is particularly vulnerable; a puncture near a joint, especially the knee, should be seen by a doctor. Any signs of purulent arthritis (redness, swelling, increasing pain, inability to move the joint through its full range of normal motion) should be considered a **medical emergency.** ● Do not remove an object, even if it is a knife blade, nail, wood, glass, or needle, from a puncture wound. Let your doctor remove it. Further damage can be caused by improper removal of the object. ● If a puncture wound remains tender for more than one or two days, it should be seen by your doctor.

DOCTOR'S TREATMENT

A puncture wound cannot be cleaned properly, even by a doctor. Your doctor will try to determine if any foreign bodies are present by feeling the wound or by X ray. Such foreign material may need to be removed surgically; or the doctor may wait and observe the wound for a while, perhaps recommending that it be soaked in Epsom salts solution for five to ten minutes four times a day. Antibiotics will be prescribed if the wound is infected, tetanus toxoid if immunization is not current. If a wound has penetrated a joint, the abdomen, chest, skull, or a tendon, your doctor will explore the wound surgically.

Puncture wounds are ideal sites for developing tetanus and are susceptible to infection.

Reye's Syndrome

DESCRIPTION

Reye's syndrome is a type of encephalitis (inflammation of the brain) that also affects the liver. It is a somewhat rare, noncontagious disease that strikes children under the age of 18, often after they are recovering from a viral infection such as influenza or chicken pox. It is most commonly seen in children between the ages of five and eleven years and most often between December and March.

Reye's syndrome is a serious disease that requires immediate treatment. It is fatal in 25 percent of all cases.

This disorder is different from other types of encephalitis because it not only causes the brain to swell but also causes fatty deposits to collect in the liver, thereby resulting in malfunctions in both organs. Brain damage, coma, or death can result if it is not diagnosed and treated quickly.

The exact cause of Reye's syndrome is not known, but since it almost always follows a viral infection, it has been theorized that the virus combines with another unknown substance in the body and produces a damaging poison.

DIAGNOSIS

The symptoms of Reye's syndrome are sudden vomiting, abnormal sleepiness or hyperactivity, and confusion. Convulsions and coma may occur as the disease progresses. Early diagnosis is crucial. Reye's syndrome is diagnosed by careful observation of the symptoms; testing of a sample of cerebrospinal fluid (the clear fluid of the central nervous system, produced in the brain) but only if there is no suspicion that there is increased pressure in the brain; blood tests to determine the presence of liver damage; and tests of the blood sugar level, because it is often low in young children who develop this disease.

HOME TREATMENT

None.

PRECAUTIONS

● There are no specific steps to prevent Reye's syndrome. However, although it has not been proven that aspirin causes or promotes Reye's syndrome, it is recommended that aspirin not be given to children with a viral infection, especially chicken pox and influenza.

DOCTOR'S TREATMENT

There is no known cure for Reye's syndrome. Treatment usually consists of helping the child to weather the first few days of the illness, maintaining normal blood sugar levels and reducing pressure on the swollen brain. Usually, if the child survives for three or four days, the symptoms will subside and recovery will follow. If blood sugar is low, normal levels should be restored with the injection of glucose, a form of sugar, into the veins. Increased pressure on the brain from the swelling is also reduced with medication.

Ringworm

DESCRIPTION

Ringworm is a misnomer. The condition does not involve a ring or a worm. It is actually a skin infection caused by a fungus. Ringworm spreads by direct contact with an infected individual or pet or by indirect contact with contaminated objects such as combs, pillows, towels, clothing, and even floors.

Different fungi prefer different areas of the body. Ringworm of the scalp (tinea capitis) appears as scaly patches on the scalp with stubs of broken-off hairs. Ringworm of the body (tinea corporis) shows up as round or oval red, scaly patches that enlarge while healing proceeds from the center. Ringworm of the groin (tinea cruris) is characterized by a red or brown scaly rash on the crotch and genital area and has a sharply defined margin of spread. Ringworm of the feet (athlete's foot; tinea pedis) affects the feet and sometimes the ankles and legs.

DIAGNOSIS

The diagnosis of ringworm is based on your child's history and on close inspection of the rash. It is confirmed by isolating and culturing the fungus and examining it under a microscope.

HOME TREATMENT

Fungicidal ointments and undecylenic acid ointments are applied until the skin clears.

PRECAUTIONS

● Several other common rashes resemble ringworm. If a rash does not improve after several days of home treatment, see your doctor. ● Treatment of ringworm may create its own rash on sensitive skin. If the rash worsens or changes in character, stop home treatment and see your doctor.

DOCTOR'S TREATMENT

Your doctor can validate your diagnosis by viewing your child's rash under ultraviolet light and by culturing and microscopically examining the results. A local fungicidal ointment or an oral fungicide may be prescribed.

Roseola

DESCRIPTION

Roseola is an acute, infectious disease—caused by an unidentified virus—that is characterized by a high fever followed by a rash. It occurs almost exclusively in infants from six months to three years of age. The incubation period for the disease is seven to seventeen days. One attack provides life-long immunity.

Roseola begins suddenly with a fever of 104°F to 106°F. It often causes convulsions at the onset but rarely any other symptoms. Sometimes, it causes a runny nose, mild redness of the throat, and minimal enlargement of the lymph nodes of the neck. Generally, the fever persists for three or four days and cannot be kept down with acetaminophen. Meanwhile, your child appears to be less ill than the degree of the fever suggests. The fever disappears abruptly; at the same time, a splotchy, red rash appears on the trunk and spreads to the child's arms and neck. When the rash disappears in one or two days, your child is well again. Complications are rare.

DIAGNOSIS

Roseola is difficult to identify until the fever drops and the rash appears. **In no other disease does a rash follow a fever.** The diagnosis is confirmed when, after one or two days, the white blood count drops below normal.

HOME TREATMENT

Give acetaminophen to help control the fever. Medication to prevent convulsions will be prescribed as needed.

PRECAUTIONS

● Another common illness that produces a high fever but few other symptoms or abnormal physical findings is infection of the urinary tract. It is most common in girls. ● Coughing, vomiting, diarrhea, discharge from the eyes or ears, and prostration are NOT associated with roseola.

DOCTOR'S TREATMENT

Through a careful physical examination, your doctor will rule out other illnesses that cause high fevers. A subnormal white blood cell count will be looked for after the first or second day to confirm the diagnosis.

Roseola occurs almost exclusively in children under the age of three.

Rubella

DESCRIPTION

Rubella, or German measles, is the mildest contagious disease of childhood, but it is a threat to an unborn fetus of a susceptible pregnant woman. Women who contract rubella during the first three months of pregnancy have a 50-50 chance of delivering an infant who has cataracts, a cleft palate, or an abnormal heart, or who is permanently deaf or mentally deficient.

Rubella is caused by a specific virus and may be transmitted by droplets, direct contact with an infected individual, or indirect contact with articles contaminated by the secretions from the nose, throat, urine, or stools. The incubation period for the disease is 14 to 21 days. One attack confers lifelong immunity.

Characteristic symptoms of rubella are swollen, tender lymph nodes in front of and behind the ears, at the base of the skull, and on the sides of the neck. In a day or two, a fine or splotchy, dark-pink rash begins on the face; it spreads over the rest of the body within 24 hours. The rash usually lasts about three days and may or may not be accompanied by a low-grade fever (100°F, oral; 101°F, rectal), slight reddening of the throat and the whites of the eyes, and mild loss of appetite.

The patient is contagious for the period from seven days before the onset of the illness until four or five days after the appearance of the rash. Infants born with rubella may be contagious for as long as a year.

DIAGNOSIS

No other disease causes a rash and tender enlargement of the particular lymph nodes involved in rubella. The diagnosis of rubella can be proved by isolation of the virus from the throat, blood, or urine cultures or by a rise in the blood level of antibodies against the rubella virus.

HOME TREATMENT

Give acetaminophen to reduce fever or discomfort. Keep your child away from pregnant women.

PRECAUTIONS

● Women should be immunized against rubella, or they should receive a blood test to be certain they are immune to the disease before becoming pregnant. If they are not immune, women should be immunized at least two months before trying to become pregnant. ● All children should be immunized against rubella. ● If a pregnant woman has been exposed to rubella, she should consult her obstetrician promptly.

DOCTOR'S TREATMENT

Doctors do not treat rubella in children but do establish the diagnosis by means of a physical examination and certain laboratory tests. They study antibody levels to confirm the diagnosis of rubella in pregnant women.

Scoliosis

DESCRIPTION

Scoliosis is also known as *curvature of the spine*. In profile a normal spine, or vertebral column, traces an S curve from top to bottom of the back; and viewed from the front or the rear, the spine is straight from side to side. In scoliosis, the vertebral column curves toward one side or the other. And that curve toward one side produces a second, compensating curve in the spine to keep the head straight.

One type of scoliosis *(idiopathic scoliosis)*, which more frequently affects girls than boys, has no known cause. It arises during adolescence and ceases to get worse when the child stops growing. The other types of scoliosis may develop at any age, and may be caused by: damage to the vertebrae due to infection; a tumor; injury; radiation therapy; abnormal development of the vertebrae or ribs; or weakness in the muscles of the trunk. Scoliosis also may result from a difference in the length of the legs. Unlike other forms of the disease, this type of scoliosis does not result in a fixed curvature of the spine; the vertebral column straightens when the child lies down.

DIAGNOSIS

When scoliosis is severe, the curvature of the spine can easily be seen when the child stands up. Even when scoliosis is mild, the curvature may be evident because the child stands in a hip-shot position with one hip more prominent than the other. Scoliosis in almost any degree can be observed when the child bends forward with his knees straight. In this position scoliosis will cause the chest to rotate, making one side of the back more prominent.

HOME TREATMENT

The important aspect of home treatment is to watch for the onset of the condition by observing your child's posture periodically, particularly during periods of rapid growth.

PRECAUTIONS

● Any evidence of curvature of the spine is abnormal. Since scoliosis can become severe in a matter of months, your child should be checked and the condition followed by a doctor.

DOCTOR'S TREATMENT

After confirming the presence of the scoliosis, your doctor will often refer you to an orthopedist. The specialist will x-ray the spine. Differences in leg length will be treated by placing lifts in shoes or by surgery.

Idiopathic scoliosis occasionally corrects itself during growth. However, it must be checked several times a year. Correction of idiopathic scoliosis may require the use of a back brace or surgery of the spine.

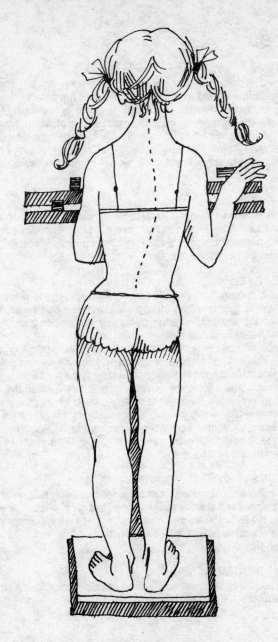

Severe scoliosis is evident when the child stands up.

Scrapes

DESCRIPTION

A scrape (abrasion) is a shallow break in the skin caused by an injury. Scrapes are distinguished from cuts and lacerations in that their depth is less than their surface length and width. Scrapes are, certainly, the most common and least dangerous injuries sustained by children. Most of them do not involve the loss of a full thickness of skin. They therefore heal with little or no scarring. However, any embedded dirt, sand, gravel, or blacktop may be permanently sealed under the skin if it is not removed before the abrasion heals.

DIAGNOSIS

Scrapes are obvious. When the surface of a scrape does not bleed uniformly, it is classified as a first- or second-degree abrasion and can be treated at home. A third-degree abrasion bleeds uniformly over its entire surface, may scar, and must be seen by a doctor.

HOME TREATMENT

To stop the bleeding, apply gentle pressure directly to the wound through a square of sterile gauze. Wash the wound with soap and water; then, look for any embedded dirt. Inspect the wound carefully under good light and, if necessary, with a magnifying glass.

If dirt is not embedded in the wound, apply a non-stinging antiseptic, cover the scrape with a sterile bandage, and keep it covered until it heals completely and the scab falls off spontaneously. If the abrasion is in an area of constant motion (at a joint, for example), periodically swab the scab with an antibiotic or antiseptic ointment to keep it pliable and to avoid cracking.

If dirt is embedded in the wound, dab anesthetic ointment on the area, then begin to scrub gently. Sometimes, residual dirt will be extruded from a wound if the abrasion is kept covered and liberal amounts of antibiotic ointment are applied twice a day.

PRECAUTIONS

● Remove dirt from an abrasion, both to guard against infection and to prevent it from being permanently sealed under the skin. ● Tetanus is unlikely, but not impossible. Since doctors seldom treat abrasions, keep the child's tetanus boosters up to date. ● Impetigo may begin at the site of an abrasion; treat accordingly.

DOCTOR'S TREATMENT

If an abrasion is deep and badly soiled your doctor will anesthetize the region and scrub out the dirt with a brush or solvent.

Inspect wounds carefully for embedded dirt.

Sinusitis

DESCRIPTION

Sinusitis is an inflammation or infection of the sinuses, the air-filled cavities in the face that connect with the nasal passages.

Because the sinuses are continuations of the nasal cavity, they are affected by any infection of the nose or any allergic reaction in the nose. Sometimes, a virus or an allergy attacks the openings to the sinuses, which induces a bacterial infection within the sinus. Sometimes, an infection of the sinus follows an infection of the nose.

The symptoms of sinusitis include fever (sometimes as high as 105°F), pain, stuffy nose, and cough. Depending on the location of the infection, headache may occur in the back of the head, at the temples and over the eyes, or above and below the eyes. Small children may develop red and swollen eyelids. But the key to identifying sinusitis is the opaque discharge from the nose.

DIAGNOSIS

With sinusitis, discharge from the nose is yellow, milky, or opaque. Pus in the sinuses can be revealed through X ray, but a thickening of the lining of the sinuses from a common cold or an allergy may be confused with it.

HOME TREATMENT

The sinuses may be protected from infection by treating a cold with oral decongestants and nose drops or by treating an allergy with oral antihistamines. Decongestants, nose drops, and antihistamines also encourage drainage after sinusitis has developed. Heat may be applied to the affected sinuses, and acetaminophen may be given to relieve the pain and fever.

PRECAUTIONS

● A high fever (103°F oral or 104°F rectal) plus signs of sinusitis indicate a potentially serious infection. See your doctor. ● Pus-like discharge or signs of sinusitis on one side of the nose suggest a foreign object may be lodged in the nose or the nose may be deformed. See your doctor.

DOCTOR'S TREATMENT

Your doctor may prescribe oral antibiotics after identifying the infecting bacteria. Suction may be used to drain the sinuses of older children with sinusitis. Surgical drainage is rarely indicated in children.

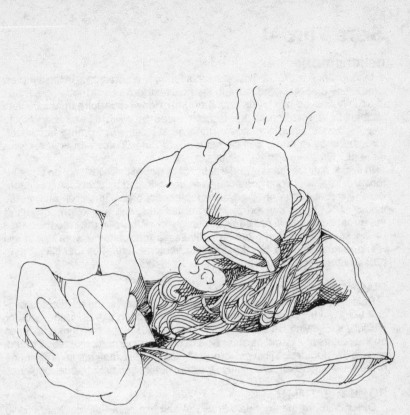

Home treatment of sinusitis can include the application of heat to the affected sinuses.

Sore Throat

DESCRIPTION

In *theory* and in the medical school classroom a sore throat is the simplest problem to diagnose and to treat. Medical textbooks state that a sore throat is usually caused by a virus and, therefore, does not require treatment with antibiotics. A sore throat that is not caused by a virus is usually due to streptococcus. Streptococcus organisms can be isolated on a throat culture, and a strep throat can be treated with penicillin or with erythromycin if the child is allergic to penicillin.

In *practice* the diagnosis and treatment of a sore throat are not so straightforward. Viral infections sometimes are complicated by streptococcal infections. A throat culture may isolate streptococci organisms even though the illness is not being caused by these organisms, and five to ten percent of the throat cultures will not show streptococci even when they are the cause of the sore throat. Some bacterial illnesses that cause a sore throat will respond to antibiotics, but the infecting bacteria cannot be identified on an ordinary throat culture plate.

DIAGNOSIS

Determining the presence of a sore throat in infants and toddlers is difficult because they cannot communicate, but swollen glands in the neck or difficulty swallowing are clues. Determining the cause of a sore throat depends on the results of a throat or other type of culture, on a complete blood count, and on the doctor's skill in performing the physical examination, knowledge of the illnesses that are prevalent in the community, and professional judgment.

HOME TREATMENT

Older children may gargle with warm salt water, but all children should drink extra fluids and eat their usual diet if they can. Give acetaminophen to reduce pain or fever and isolate the child from other children, particularly infants, until the cause of the problem is found.

PRECAUTIONS

● Take the child to a doctor if a sore throat is accompanied by any of the following symptoms: moderately or severely swollen and tender neck glands; difficulty swallowing that cannot be relieved by acetaminophen; pus-like discharge from the eyes or nose; moderate or severe earache; tenderness over the sinuses; difficulty breathing; chest pain; reddish-purple rash or a rash resembling scarlet fever; stiff neck; prostration; disorientation; or continual vomiting. ● If a sore throat and a fever continue to worsen after 24 to 36 hours, consult a doctor.

DOCTOR'S TREATMENT

Your doctor will conduct a complete physical examination and order a throat culture and, perhaps, other laboratory tests. Depending on the results, your doctor may elect to treat a sore throat with antibiotics. Regardless of the treatment prescribed, you should report any new symptoms or lack of improvement after 24 hours to your doctor.

Speech Problems & Stuttering

DESCRIPTION

Children learn to speak by imitation. But they may learn at different rates depending on their intelligence, hearing, and their control of the muscles involved in speaking. And speech may be delayed or impaired if their speech centers in the brain or their larynx, throat, nose, tongue, or lips are not normal.

Learning to speak depends on how often a child hears speech, how well he is motivated to speak, and how much he is encouraged to speak. On the average a baby begins to babble and make sounds at four to six months of age. By eight months, he has achieved a typical baby vocabulary using such "words" as "goo," "ba-ba," and "da-da." By 12 months, a baby will be using two-syllable "words" meaningfully ("ma-ma" for mother, "ba-ba" for bottle), and by two years old will be connecting words purposefully ("go bye-bye," "want cookie"). A child of five years can speak five-word sentences, and a child of six can make all the sounds of the alphabet, except perhaps the sounds for s and z.

Children from age two to five often lack fluency, and they may stutter or stammer at times. If the lack of fluency or stuttering or stammering continues the child may have a speech problem. Or if speech does not develop normally it may be due to partial or complete deafness, mental retardation, inadequate exposure to language, brain damage, anatomical abnormalities, or malfunction of the speech centers (aphasia).

DIAGNOSIS

Any marked delay in a child's achieving speech raises the suspicion of a speech problem.

HOME TREATMENT

To learn to speak adequately, your baby must be spoken to *and* listened to. Improper speech should be corrected, but a child should not be chastised, deliberately ignored, or forced to practice speaking. Stuttering in children aged two to five may be disregarded unless it is still a problem several months after its onset. It should not provoke anger or anxiety, suggestions that the child speak more slowly or more clearly, or laughter and taunts from siblings. Stuttering warrants professional attention if it is severe, constant, or prolonged.

PRECAUTIONS

● If your child's speech does not develop more or less in accordance with the timetable above, consult your doctor. ● Do not refuse to understand your child or force him to speak more clearly. ● Do not call the child's attention to his stuttering. Read, sing, and speak to your child whenever possible. Notice if your child speaks only in a monotone or with a marked nasal quality or if his vocabulary and his ability to pronounce words are diminishing instead of improving.

continued

DOCTOR'S TREATMENT

Your doctor will perform a complete physical examination, checking the throat, palate, and tongue and testing your child's hearing. If your child is under the age of five you may be referred to a speech pathologist for evaluation and treatment if: stuttering is severe, constant, or unduly prolonged; the child seems to be severely frustrated; or if you need assistance in handling your child's development of speech. If your child substitutes sounds or stutters after the age of five or six, your doctor may suggest he be seen by a speech specialist.

Children who stutter after the age of five may need to see a speech specialist.

Sprains & Dislocations

DESCRIPTION

All joints of the body are surrounded by ligaments, which can be partially or completely torn when the joint is forcibly twisted beyond its normal range of motion. A partially or completely torn ligament is called a *sprain,* and it causes pain (sometimes severe), swelling, tenderness, decreased motion of the joint, and internal bleeding.

If ligaments are badly torn the bones of the joint may slip out of position or become dislocated. Besides the usual symptoms of a sprain, a *dislocation* causes gross deformity and marked or total loss of function of the dislocated parts. Even after the dislocation has been corrected, the joint remains unstable for weeks.

Sprains are common during childhood, but dislocations other than a dislocated elbow (Malgaigne's luxation of the elbow) are rare. Sprains most often occur in the fingers (called "jammed" or "baseball" fingers), toes, ankles, neck, and back. Dislocations can also occur in the fingers, toes, kneecaps, and shoulders.

DIAGNOSIS

Because dislocations produce gross deformity, they seldom are missed. Sprains, if mild or moderate, generally can be suspected if a joint is tender after it has been twisted or overextended. Fractures of the bones of the involved joint cannot be ruled out without X rays.

HOME TREATMENT

A dislocation should not be treated at home. Mild sprains, particularly of the fingers, toes, and ankles, may be treated safely at home by splinting and avoiding use of the involved hand or foot. The sprained part should be elevated, and cold compresses can be applied for one to four hours after injury to minimize swelling. Acetaminophen will temporarily relieve pain. If a sprain does not improve rapidly a bone may be fractured; the child should be seen by a doctor.

PRECAUTIONS

● Do not attempt to correct a dislocation, even of the fingers. Dislocations are often accompanied by a fracture. ● An apparently sprained wrist in a child actually may be a fracture of the forearm bones near the joint and a sprained thumb actually may be a fractured navicular bone. ● A severe sprain may take as long as a fracture to heal and if it is not treated properly can result in a permanently weak joint. ● A sprain is not healed if it is still swollen or if it is painful to move. ● Elastic bandages do not adequately support or protect a sprained ankle.

continued

DOCTOR'S TREATMENT

Your doctor will carefully examine all the anatomical parts of the injured joint and take X rays if a dislocation or a bad sprain is suspected. A minor sprain may be x-rayed or the joint immobilized and its rate of healing observed. If the rate of healing is not rapid enough an X ray will be ordered.

Treatment for a sprained joint may include elevation and immobilization.

Stomach Ache, Acute

DESCRIPTION

The abdomen contains the stomach, small and large intestines, liver, spleen, pancreas, kidneys, urinary bladder, gallbladder, and the organs of reproduction. Disease or injury of any of these organs can cause abdominal pain. Consequently, a "stomach ache" can test the diagnostic mettle of a parent or a doctor. Fortunately, almost all stomach aches in children are caused by one of four problems: constipation, acute gastrointestinal upset (caused by viruses, bacteria, or dietary indiscretion), emotional stress, or urinary tract infection.

Other, less frequent causes of a stomach ache are: appendicitis, acute abdominal pain from pneumonia, mononucleosis, and hepatitis.

DIAGNOSIS

The diagnosis first involves ruling out appendicitis. If appendicitis can be ruled out, then consider that:

Your child probably is *constipated* if he has not had a bowel movement or has had a hard one recently; if the pain is intermittent (crampy) on the left side of the body and follows eating; and if the abdomen is soft and not tender.

Your child probably has *gastrointestinal upset* if he has been exposed to someone else who has acute gastroenteritis or if he has eaten too much; if the pain is intermittent and occurs around the upper abdomen or umbilicus; or if diarrhea follows vomiting.

Your child's stomach ache is probably due to *emotional stress* if he is or has been upset and if the pain does not worsen.

If your child's pain cannot be explained by any of these causes take him to your doctor.

Your child's stomach ache probably is due to *urinary tract infection* if the pain is low in the belly or generalized and intermittent; or if he has a fever and frequent, painful urination.

HOME TREATMENT

Unless severe (acute pain lasting for more than 24 hours), gastrointestinal upset will go away on its own, but an antiemetic can relieve the vomiting, and mild heat applied to the abdomen can relieve the pain. A stomach ache due to emotional stress will ease with relief from the stress, but one that arises from urinary tract infection requires the attention of a physician. If stomach pain persists or worsens take your child to your doctor.

PRECAUTIONS

● Never give a child a laxative or place ice on the abdomen to treat abdominal pain. ● Steady, worsening pain usually is more serious than intermittent, crampy pain; but severe, regular, crampy pain may indicate a serious problem, particularly if it accompanies blood or mucus in the stools. ● Abdominal pain that forces a child to bend forward as he walks is a cause for concern. ● Abdominal pain combined with a fever and a cough suggests

continued

pneumonia. ● Severe, worsening abdominal pain that follows an injury to the abdomen or lower chest suggests internal injury.

DOCTOR'S TREATMENT

Your doctor's first task is to determine the cause of the pain by taking a detailed history, performing a complete physical examination, and (often) conducting a battery of laboratory tests or X rays. If the diagnosis remains doubtful your doctor may observe your child for a few hours or ask for a consultation with another physician.

Too many green apples can cause acute stomach pain.

Stomach Ache, Chronic

DESCRIPTION
Chronic stomach pain usually is due to constipation, intolerance of cow's milk (lactase deficiency), or emotional stress. Other, less common causes are: urinary tract problems (obstruction, chronic infection); peptic ulcer; sickle cell anemia; lead poisoning; ulcerative colitis; regional enteritis (Crohn's disease); tumors; ovarian problems; worm infestations (pinworms, Giardia); intolerance of foods other than milk; and internal hernias.

DIAGNOSIS
Recurrent abdominal pain is not due to appendicitis. To pinpoint its cause, recurrent abdominal pain must be associated with other symptoms such as: vomiting; diarrhea; constipation; blood or mucus in the stools; fever; failure to gain weight; painful urination; ingesting inedible substances (pica); or anemia. Also important is the pattern of the pain—where it is, how long it lasts, and when it occurs.

In general, recurrent abdominal pain that is accompanied by no other symptoms or that has no set pattern is probably not serious.

HOME TREATMENT
If emotional stress is responsible for the stomach ache, try to eliminate the stress. Most important, note and record the pattern of recurrent abdominal pain and any other symptoms that occur before consulting your doctor.

PRECAUTIONS
● Recurrent abdominal pain from emotional stress is real and requires treatment just as much as the pain of an ulcer, ileitis, or colitis.

DOCTOR'S TREATMENT
Your doctor will take a careful history of your child's recent health and perform a complete physical examination. A urinalysis and urine culture, blood tests, and stool examinations will often be ordered. If the cause of the pain still is not clear, X rays of the stomach, large and small bowels, and the urinary tract may be required. If X rays provide no clues to the problem, your child may be hospitalized for extensive blood tests and internal abdominal examination (endoscopy or laparoscopy).

Strep Throat

DESCRIPTION

Strep throat is a highly contagious infection of the throat usually due to the group A strain of beta-hemolytic streptococci. Although some strep germs do not cause rashes, most types can produce a toxin that causes the rash that typifies *scarlet fever* (also commonly called *scarlatina).* There are at least 60 different types of streptococcus organisms. After an attack of strep throat the individual is immune to further attack from that one type of streptococcus organism only. But once a person has had strep with a rash, he is immune to the rash for a lifetime. With or without a rash, strep throat is a serious illness.

The incubation period of strep throat is two to five days, and it is passed from child to child through the oral or nasal secretions from an infected individual, or it may be spread by a carrier who has no symptoms of the illness. At times, as many as half the children in any one area may be carriers of the disease.

The onset of strep throat is sudden. It begins with a headache, fever up to 104°F, sore and spotted throat, vomiting, abdominal pain, swollen lymph nodes in the neck, and prostration. If the infecting organism is rash-producing and the child is not immune, he will develop a rash within 24 to 72 hours. The rash is typical with fine, slightly raised red spots resembling coarse red sandpaper. It appears on the base of the neck, in the armpits and groin, and then on the trunk and extremities. The child's face is flushed, but his lips are pale. When the rash subsides in three to twenty days, the skin flakes and peels.

A streptococcal infection **can be serious.** Among its complications are rheumatic fever, nephritis, middle ear infection, sinusitis, pneumonia, and transient arthritis.

DIAGNOSIS

The diagnosis of a strep throat cannot be confirmed without a throat culture that isolates streptococcus organisms. However, cultures are only 90 to 95 percent reliable. The diagnosis of scarlet fever is based on the appearance of the rash.

HOME TREATMENT

No home treatment is recommended except to alleviate the pain and fever with acetaminophen. Streptococcal infections should be treated by your doctor.

PRECAUTIONS

● Infants are immune to the scarlet fever toxin for four to six months if their mothers are immune. They are NOT immune to a streptococcal infection, which may be very serious but may not produce typical symptoms. Consequently, keep infants away from groups of children, some of whom may be carriers of streptococci. ● If one child in your family has a streptococcal infection, watch your other children for signs of infection. ● Follow the full course of antibiotic therapy prescribed by a doctor, giving your child the medication until it is gone.

DOCTOR'S TREATMENT

Strep throat is diagnosed by means of a physical examination and the results of a culture. Penicillin (or another antibiotic for those who are allergic to penicillin) is usually prescribed for 10 days to cure the streptococcal infection. Antibiotics prevent rheumatic fever and *may* prevent nephritis. A child who develops complications may have to be hospitalized.

To help diagnose a strep throat a doctor will take a throat culture to determine the presence of streptococci.

Styes

DESCRIPTION

Styes are boils of the oil or sweat glands in the upper or lower eyelids. Usually, they are caused by staphylococcus organisms, and they may spread from individual to individual through direct contact. Styes tend to occur in crops because their pus contains staphylococci that may infect other glands in the eyelids.

Styes develop like boils. The area at the edge of the eyelid becomes increasingly red, painful, tender, and swollen. After two to three days, pus forms, and the stye "points"; that is, a yellow head appears at the edge of the lid near the base of the eyelashes. Styes usually break spontaneously, drain, and heal. Occasionally, a stye will heal without pointing or draining.

DIAGNOSIS

Styes differ from insect bites and cysts because they are painful, tender swellings near the margins of the eyelids that usually come to a head. Insect bites itch, are not painful, and do not come to a head. Cysts are lumps or swellings that show through the undersurface of the eyelids as pink or pale-yellow spots. Unless infected, they are not tender. Unlike styes, cysts do not come to a head, and they persist for some time.

HOME TREATMENT

Place warm soaks (using cotton balls or a washcloth) on the eyelids several times a day for 10 to 20 minutes each time. Give acetaminophen to reduce pain. Administer antibiotic eye drops several times a day to prevent the formation of additional styes.

PRECAUTIONS

● The whites of the eyes do not become red as a result of a stye. ● One large, or several small, recurring styes, or a stye that accompanies such symptoms as fever, headache, loss of appetite, or lethargy should be seen by a doctor. ● Styes are somewhat contagious. Keep an infected child's towel and washcloth separate.

DOCTOR'S TREATMENT

To treat one large or several small, recurring styes, your doctor may prescribe antibiotics. A stye will rarely be incised and drained. A culture of the nose and throat may be taken to ascertain the source of the staphylococci. As a last resort, your doctor may administer an immunization against staphylococci each week.

Treat styes with warm soaks on the eyelids.

Sunburn

DESCRIPTION

Sunburn is a thermal burn, usually of the first degree. Occasionally, a sunburn causes a skin rash which resembles hives or poison ivy. This condition is called sun poisoning. Babies and children who have fair complexions are particularly susceptible to sunburn, even on cloudy days or in shade.

DIAGNOSIS

The diagnosis of sunburn generally is immediately obvious. Sun poisoning, however, may not appear for several days.

HOME TREATMENT

Apply cocoa butter, commercial burn ointments, cold water compresses, or a baking-soda-and-tap-water paste to the burn. Do not break blisters. Give aspirin or acetaminophen to relieve pain and antihistamines to reduce itching.

PRECAUTIONS

● The most important aspect of home treatment is prevention. ● Apply sunscreens to filter out damaging rays of the sun, but remember that sunscreens do not permit unlimited exposure. And remember that all sunscreens wash off with swimming and perspiration. Follow the instructions on the product's package for reapplying the sunscreen. ● Sunscreens may cause a mild rash on some people. If a rash appears, switch to another product. ● Medication applied to large sunburn areas (anesthetics in burn ointments or steroids) may be absorbed into the body and produce side effects. Use such medication sparingly. ● Injury to the skin from overexposure to ultraviolet light from sunlamps is common among teenagers. ● Some medications (for example, tetracycline and its derivatives, chlorpromazine, griseofulvin and coal tar ointments) increase the sensitivity of the skin to sunburn. ● Take the child to a doctor if he has a sunburn plus a fever or prostration.

DOCTOR'S TREATMENT

Your doctor may prescribe oral or spray steroids to treat your child's sunburn or sun poisoning. A child who has a severe burn will be hospitalized for treatment.

Apply sunscreens before your child goes out in the sun.

Swallowed Objects

DESCRIPTION

Over 95 percent of the penny-, nickel-, or dime-size foreign objects that are swallowed by children cause no trouble and pass from the body in the stools. But objects that are the size of a quarter or larger may become lodged in the esophagus; sharp objects (pins, needles, bones, matchsticks, nails, glass splinters) may lodge in the tonsils, throat, or esophagus; and objects longer than a toothpick may not be able to pass out of the stomach.

Depending on where the object is lodged, it may cause gagging, pain, or discomfort in the throat or chest, or difficulty swallowing. Once a foreign object passes into the stomach, it does not produce any symptoms unless it obstructs or penetrates the digestive tract. Then, abdominal pain, vomiting, and fever may develop.

DIAGNOSIS

Metallic objects are visible on an X ray, but those made of wood, plastic, or glass are not. Usually, however, the diagnosis is suggested by the circumstances and whatever symptoms of the above there may be.

HOME TREATMENT

No treatment is necessary if the swallowed object is small and smooth. If the object is long, sharp, or large, examine the stools carefully for several days to be sure it has passed from the body. Each bowel movement must be passed through a sieve. If the child has been potty trained, place in the toilet bowl a basin fashioned of window screening. Then, after the child has passed a stool wash it through the screening with hot water.

PRECAUTIONS

● An object lodged in the esophagus must be removed within hours by a doctor. ● No known food, drink, or medication will accelerate or make safer the passage of a foreign object through the body. ● If an object has not passed from the child's body within one week, notify your doctor. ● Try to bring a duplicate of the object when consulting your doctor. ● Do not give your child a laxative until the object has passed.

DOCTOR'S TREATMENT

Your doctor will carefully inspect the throat and observe the way your child swallows. X rays of the throat, neck, chest, or abdomen may be ordered. If an object is wedged in the throat or esophagus, your doctor will remove it with an instrument. If it is in the stomach, he will monitor the child's condition for three or more weeks before trying to remove it surgically. If the object is in the intestines and does not pass in one week the doctor may remove it surgically.

If the swallowed object is small and blunt, it will usually cause no problem.

Swimmer's Ear

DESCRIPTION

Irritation or infection of the external ear canal is known as swimmer's ear. Swimmer's ear may arise from a middle ear infection that has caused the eardrum to rupture and pus to drain into the external canal. Or it may follow an injury to the ear canal, which has become infected. Usually, however, it develops from swimming in fresh water or pools. Frequent and sustained moisture in the ear softens, swells, and cracks the ear canal and allows germs to penetrate and bring on infection.

A mild case of swimmer's ear may appear as an itching, clogged ear canal with or without odorous discharge; hearing may be diminished. A severe case may induce intense pain, fever, and swollen and tender lymph nodes in front of, behind, and below the ear.

DIAGNOSIS

The presence of discharge in or oozing out of the ear canal suggests swimmer's ear. Without discharge from the ear, the diagnosis is based on internal examination of the ear.

HOME TREATMENT

With your doctor's direction, administer eardrops containing antibiotics and steroids four times a day to treat a mild case of swimmer's ear. Give aspirin or acetaminophen or apply heat to the outside of the ear to reduce pain. If your child has had several bouts of swimmer's ear, drying the ear canals at the end of each day of swimming by instilling a few drops of rubbing alcohol or glycerine may prevent swimmer's ear.

PRECAUTIONS

● If a child has severe pain, fever, or swollen glands, or if he does not respond to home treatment in a few days, take him to your doctor. ● Rubber earplugs will not keep water out of the ear canals. But earplugs fashioned at home from lamb's wool and coated with petroleum jelly may. ● Do not clean ear canals by using bobby pins, swabs, or anything other than a fingertip covered with a facecloth. ● If eardrops do not penetrate deeply into the ear canal, they will not be effective. After administering the drops, be sure to keep the child's head tilted upward.

DOCTOR'S TREATMENT

In addition to eardrops your doctor may prescribe oral antibiotics. The ear canal will be cleaned if the ear is not too tender. A child who has a severe case of swimmer's ear will be hospitalized.

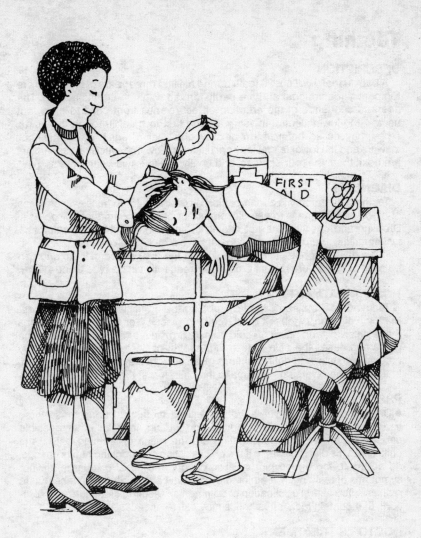

Your doctor will treat a mild case of swimmer's ear with eardrops containing antibiotics or steroids.

Teething

DESCRIPTION

A baby usually will cut 20 teeth during his first three years of life. All 20 are temporary (deciduous) and are partly formed within the gums at birth. The age and sequence of the eruption of teeth varies from child to child, but usually the lower central incisors are the first to break through the gums. (They may do so before birth or after one year of age.) The upper four incisors and the lower lateral incisors usually follow. The four one-year molars are next; then, the four canines; and finally, the four two-year molars.

DIAGNOSIS

Teething commonly is accompanied by drooling, fretfulness, wakefulness at night, unwillingness to eat, discomfort, or chewing on fingers or objects. Drooling and chewing are not related to any abnormality; and fretfulness, wakefulness, and unwillingness to eat have a multitude of causes.

A few days before teeth erupt, they push the gum ahead of them and can be seen or felt. Before molars erupt, they frequently elicit a blue blood-blister.

HOME TREATMENT

Teething pain may be eased by rubbing the gums, with or without anesthetics. Biting on zwieback toast, teething biscuits, or teething rings helps the teeth erupt, and biting on cold objects (frozen teething rings) numbs the gums and eases the pain of teething. Aspirin or acetaminophen also may help relieve pain, and antihistamines given at night may help the child sleep. In the daytime diversions may make the child forget the pain.

PRECAUTIONS

● On and off for three years, infants will be teething. During these three years, do not blame every symptom on teething; look for other possible causes. ● Diarrhea and constipation are the result of teething only if the child alters his diet radically. ● If the child's eating and drinking habits change, do not try to force-feed him. ● Fever, cough, and nasal discharge are not symptoms of teething. ● Teething may produce chapping on the face but no rashes. ● Too liberal application of commercial teething ointments and solutions that contain local anesthetics may cause anemia.

DOCTOR'S TREATMENT

Before attributing symptoms to teething, your doctor will check for other causes.

Biting on a frozen teething ring will ease the pain of teething.

Testicle, Torsion of

DESCRIPTION

For unknown reasons, a testicle may become twisted, shutting off the blood supply. Although the condition is more apt to affect boys with an undescended testicle, it is not rare among boys whose testes are in the normal position in the scrotum. The condition also may follow a minor injury.

Once a testicle has been twisted, it becomes slightly swollen and tender. A few hours later it is intensely painful, markedly tender, and swollen. The testicle and the skin surrounding it become discolored (red or blue), and the boy may be nauseated or vomit and have lower abdominal pain and a fever.

DIAGNOSIS

Torsion of a testicle that has descended into the scrotum may be confused with an infection (orchitis), a strangulated hernia, or a bruise of the scrotum. Torsion of a testicle that has *not* descended and lies in the groin may be confused with a strangulated hernia, injury, or infected lymph nodes in the groin. Torsion of an undescended testicle that lies within the abdominal cavity is difficult to diagnose but may be suspected whenever abdominal pain occurs. This condition represents an **emergency situation** and medical intervention should be immediate.

Torsion of a part of a testicle (appendix of the testis) causes similar, although less intense, symptoms of torsion of the entire testicle. Distinguishing between these conditions is unimportant because they are treated the same way.

HOME TREATMENT

None. **Torsion of the testicle is a surgical emergency.**

PRECAUTIONS

● Take your boy to a doctor immediately if pain near a testicle increases and the testicle is tender, swollen, or discolored. **Hours count.** ● Suspect torsion of the testicle in a boy with an uncorrected, undescended testicle if he has lower abdominal pain or pain in the groin. ● An injury or a bruise of the scrotum and testis is not uncommon and will cause instant pain that gradually subsides. If pain increases following an injury or a bruise suspect torsion of the testicle.

DOCTOR'S TREATMENT

Your doctor will arrange immediate surgery to untwist the testicle and anchor it in the scrotum to prevent further episodes. If surgery is not performed within 24 hours of the onset of the symptoms the testis may be damaged permanently.

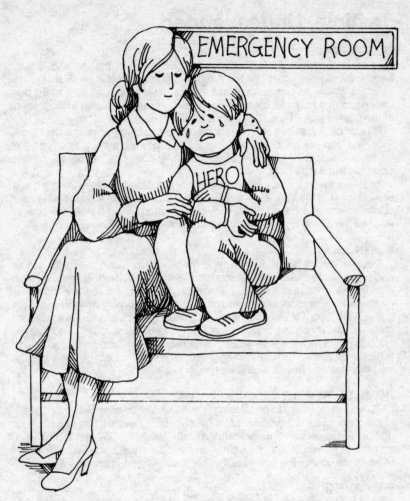

Torsion of the testicle causes intense pain and requires immediate medical attention.

Testicle, Undescended

DESCRIPTION

In the male fetus the two testicles lie just beneath the kidneys. Before birth, they migrate down into the groin and come to rest in each side of the scrotum. In one to two percent of full-term male infants and 20 to 30 percent of premature male infants the testes have not completed their descent at the time of birth. These boys have an undescended testicle.

One or both testicles may be undescended, and the undescended testis may lie within the abdomen or the groin. In a boy's first months or years of life an undescended testicle may successfully complete its migration to the scrotum. But it may not.

A testicle that remains undescended is at risk of becoming twisted, injured, or malignant. If the condition is not corrected by the time a boy reaches age seven, an undescended testicle may be damaged by the heat of the body; it may shrivel (atrophy) and lose its ability to produce sperm.

DIAGNOSIS

If one or both testicles do not rest in the scrotum at birth, the infant has an undescended testicle. An undescended testicle must be distinguished from a migratory or retractile testis, however. A migrating or retractile testis has completed its descent into the scrotum, but it temporarily has risen into the groin. A migratory or retractile testis returns to its normal position as the boy matures, and it needs no correction. If the size of the scrotum is normal the testis is migrating; if it is small the testis is undescended. An undescended testicle sometimes can be felt lying along the inguinal canal, but it may be mistaken for a hernia or a swollen lymph node.

HOME TREATMENT

If a testicle appears to be missing from the scrotum after birth, periodically check to see if it descends of its own accord. If it does not, consult your doctor. To check for an undescended testis place the boy in a tub of warm water and pull his knees up toward his chest. If the testicle is migratory it will often descend into the scrotum. If the testicle is undescended it will not.

PRECAUTIONS

● Don't worry a boy by discussing the condition. An undescended testicle usually can be corrected. ● Do not postpone correction of an undescended testicle. It should be corrected when the boy is between four and seven years old.

DOCTOR'S TREATMENT

Your doctor will examine your boy's scrotum and groin carefully and check for the presence of a hernia, which often coexists with an undescended testis. Some doctors give hormone injections to encourage descent of the testicle, but most prefer to perform surgery between the ages of four and seven without using hormones.

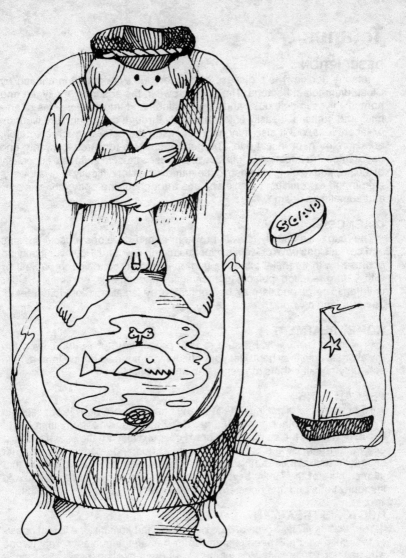

An undescended testicle should be corrected when the boy is between four and seven years old.

Tetanus

DESCRIPTION

Tetanus (lockjaw) is a disease of the nervous system that is caused by Clostridium tetani bacteria. The germ grows in the absence of oxygen and normally lives in soil, dust, and the intestines and intestinal wastes of animals and humans. It easily enters the body through deep puncture wounds or lacerations, but it also may gain access to the body through a scratch, abrasion, burn, or insect bite. The germ incubates for three to twenty-one days. Once the infection is full-blown, it causes muscle stiffness, especially of the jaw and neck (giving rise to the name lockjaw); difficulty in swallowing; pain in the extremities; muscle spasms throughout the body; convulsions; and sometimes death.

DIAGNOSIS

The diagnosis usually is evident when a child develops muscle spasms and convulsions days or weeks after sustaining a wound. However it may be confused with neonatal tetany (a generally benign condition in babies) or with a drug reaction, poisoning, meningitis, encephalitis, or rabies in older children. The diagnosis may be confirmed by isolating Clostridium tetani bacteria from a wound.

HOME TREATMENT

Prevention is the key. Be sure to take proper care of wounds, even the trivial ones, until they heal. Get your children immunized during infancy and schedule booster shots to ensure immunity for life.

PRECAUTIONS

● If a new mother is not immune to tetanus her newborn baby is susceptible to tetanus. If a mother is immune her baby may be temporarily immune to it. ● In newborns the stump of the umbilical cord may be the site of tetanus' entry into the body. If a baby is delivered at home, be certain to use strict antiseptic techniques during and immediately after birth. ● Be certain that all members of the family have received the initial series of tetanus toxoid immunizations and that boosters are given every 10 years throughout life.

DOCTOR'S TREATMENT

Your doctor will take prompt care of wounds and administer a toxoid booster to a child who has been immunized or human tetanus antiserum to one who has not. If tetanus has developed, your doctor will hospitalize your child and order intensive treatment involving antiserum, antibiotics, sedation, anesthesia, and intravenous fluids. When recovered, your child should be immunized against any subsequent attack.

Infants should be immunized against tetanus and have boosters to ensure immunity.

Tonsillitis

DESCRIPTION

The tonsils (in the throat) and the adenoids (in the back of the nose) are part of the lymphatic system; their function is to destroy disease-causing germs. They may also become mildly or chronically infected.

Chronic or recurrent infections of the tonsils and adenoids can result in their permanent enlargement (hypertrophy). Enlargement of the tonsils rarely produces symptoms by itself but, in extreme cases, it may interfere with swallowing. Enlargement of the adenoids results in mouth breathing, hearing loss and middle ear infection, snoring, nasal speech, and bad breath.

A unique infection of the tonsils is quinsy sore throat (peritonsillar abscess). A large abscess forms behind a tonsil, producing intense pain and a high fever (103°F or 104°F). The abscess eventually pushes the tonsil across the midline of the throat.

DIAGNOSIS

Acute infection of the tonsils is diagnosed on the basis of the appearance of the throat and the results of a throat culture or blood count. Chronic infection of the adenoids and tonsils is diagnosed on the basis of frequent bouts of infection or almost constant symptoms of infection and the presence of chronically swollen lymph nodes in the neck. Enlarged tonsils can be observed in the throat, but they must not be mistaken for temporarily enlarged tonsils due to acute infection. Enlarged adenoids cannot be seen directly. Special instruments must be used or X rays may be taken.

HOME TREATMENT

Treatment of tonsillitis is the same as treatment of the common cold, sore throat, or hay fever. A peritonsillar abscess requires treatment by a doctor.

PRECAUTIONS

● Adenoids and tonsils usually are large in children three to nine years of age. Do not confuse this enlargement with one of chronic infection. ● Tonsils often contain a white, cheesy material. This material is normal; it does not indicate infection. ● Tonsils and adenoids may be chronically infected without becoming enlarged. A history of recurring infection and the condition of the lymph nodes in the neck are more reliable indicators of chronic infection than size.

DOCTOR'S TREATMENT

Your doctor will treat a peritonsillar abscess with antibiotics; occasionally surgical drainage is necessary.

The decision to remove tonsils and adenoids surgically requires considerable evaluation. Tonsillectomy may be performed as part of the treatment of: a peritonsillar abscess or frequent infections (for more than a year) of the tonsils; a tonsillar tumor; or a diphtheria bacilli-infected tonsil.

Adenoidectomy may be performed to correct: a nasal obstruction that has led to facial peculiarities such as a pinched face, narrow nostrils, or constantly open mouth; a chronic cough; bad breath; snoring; or a nasal voice. It also may be wise to have adenoids removed if their enlargement is causing a hearing loss or frequent middle ear infections. Or it may be done as part of the treatment of frequent infections of the adenoids.

Mild tonsillitis can be treated in the same way a sore throat is treated.

Urinary Tract Infection

DESCRIPTION

Infections of the urinary tract are common during childhood, and they are 10 times more frequent in girls than in boys. About five percent of all girls will have one or more urinary tract infections before reaching maturity.

In most cases, except during infancy, no physical abnormality accounts for the development of a urinary tract infection (UTI). But for five percent of the girls and over 50 percent of the boys with UTI, an underlying anatomical abnormality somewhere along the urinary tract results in a partial or total block in the flow of urine. Most UTIs are caused by germs, such as E. coli bacilli, that do not cause disease in other locations. E. coli bacilli live peacefully in the bowels of all children and adults but cause infection when they ascend the urethra (the tube that leads to the urinary bladder). Other causes of UTI are inflammation of the vagina, foreign bodies in the bladder or urethra, and possibly severe constipation.

The urinary tract is a series of interconnected tubes; an infection in one part easily spreads to another. A urinary tract infection may elicit no symptoms at all (silent UTI) or any combination of the following: urgency, frequency, or pain on urination; dribbling of urine; bedwetting; daytime incontinence; foul-smelling, cloudy, or bloody urine; fever; abdominal or back pain; vomiting; and redness of the external genitalia. If the infection goes untreated, the symptoms generally disappear in a few days or weeks and often return later.

DIAGNOSIS

The diagnosis of UTI depends upon a careful physical examination and urinalysis and urine culture. In boys, the diagnosis involves a search for an obstruction in the urinary tract. In girls, the search for an obstruction is undertaken only after two or three bouts of UTI or one bout with an infection that is resistant to treatment. In infants, investigation for the underlying cause is always undertaken immediately.

HOME TREATMENT

Any attempt to treat UTI at home is potentially dangerous and may result in a low-grade, destructive infection with no outward symptoms.

PRECAUTIONS

● Fever, but few or no other symptoms, and a normal physical examination are a common UTI profile, particularly if it is a recurrent pattern. ● To obtain a urine specimen for analysis or culture, cleanse the genitalia and collect the portion at the midpoint of urination. In this way, the urine sample will not be contaminated.

DOCTOR'S TREATMENT

Your doctor will conduct a complete physical examination, including measurement of your child's blood pressure, urinalysis, and urine culture. Appropriate antibiotics will be prescribed for 10 to 14 days. Urine samples will be tested during and after the course of antibiotics.

After your child has recovered from a UTI, your doctor may recommend X rays to rule out a physical abnormality. Sometimes, further X rays and direct examination of urethra and bladder are necessary. To treat recurrent UTIs that are not due to obstruction, your doctor may prescribe the use of antibiotics—constantly or intermittently for months or years. To correct an obstruction, your doctor will perform surgery.

Girls are much more likely to suffer urinary tract infections than are boys.

Vomiting

DESCRIPTION

Vomiting is a common occurrence during childhood. In most instances, it is merely a nuisance, but at times it can hinder the work of medications or promote dehydration through the loss of fluids.

Most infants spit up and occasionally vomit. If vomiting does not hinder weight gain, it is neither harmful nor abnormal. Excessive vomiting, however, may indicate an intolerance to formula, milk, or some foods. Frequent, forceful vomiting during an infant's first month suggests an obstruction at the end of the stomach.

In children, a viral infection of the digestive tract (gastroenteritis or intestinal flu) or an infectious disease elsewhere in the body can cause vomiting. Less common causes are abnormalities of the brain (concussion, migraine, meningitis, encephalitis, tumors); poisoning; appendicitis; severe emotional distress; jaundice; foreign bodies in the digestive tract; abdominal injuries; and motion sickness.

DIAGNOSIS

The diagnosis is determined by identifying the reason for the vomiting. Another important factor is evaluating the degree of dehydration caused by persistent vomiting.

HOME TREATMENT

When your child is vomiting, do not give him solid foods, milk, or oral aspirin; they aggravate vomiting. Do allow him sips of cold, clear liquids (ice chips, carbonated beverages, tea with sugar, liquid gelatin dessert, water, mineral and electrolyte solutions, and apple juice are good). Commercial preparations of orthophosphoric acid, fructose, and glucose also may be given. If a teaspoon of liquid is retained every five minutes, two ounces of fluid will be retained in an hour.

Some physicians warn against the use of antiemetic medications because they may obscure the diagnosis and possibly provoke Reye's syndrome (characterized by swelling of the brain and enlargement of the liver). However, dimenhydrinate in liquid or tablet form is recommended by thousands of practicing physicians, and it has effectively prevented dehydration in many children. (The drug is most effective if nothing is taken by mouth for at least an hour after the first dose. The drug should be repeated every four hours.)

PRECAUTIONS

● Watch for signs of dehydration in your child. ● Medication to relieve diarrhea often aggravates vomiting. If vomiting and diarrhea are happening simultaneously, treat the vomiting until it stops; then treat the diarrhea. ● Some phenothiazines that are used to stop vomiting in adults may cause serious central nervous system side effects in children; do not use them for children. Remember that abdominal pain (with or without vomiting) is appendicitis until proved otherwise.

DOCTOR'S TREATMENT

Your doctor will determine the cause of vomiting by obtaining a detailed history and performing a careful physical and neurological examination. The presence and degree of dehydration will be assessed and your child hospitalized for administration of intravenous fluids if the condition is serious. Chlorpromazine or dimenhydrinate may be prescribed to relieve vomiting.

Give your child sips of sugared tea or cold, clear liquids.

Warts

DESCRIPTION

A wart is a growth on the skin caused by a specific virus. Although warts may differ in appearance, they are caused by the same virus. The *common wart* is an ordinary, rough, raised wart that ranges in size from one-eighth to one inch and occurs anywhere on the skin. A *juvenile wart* is a small (one-sixteenth to one-fourth inch), smooth, pinkish wart that is common on the hands. Warts on the soles of the feet are *plantar warts.* They may be pressed into the foot (sometimes to a depth of a quarter inch or more) and often are surrounded by a callus. Groups of plantar warts are known as "mosaic warts."

Warts can be spread by direct contact or by scratching. Plantar warts can also be contracted by walking barefooted where someone who has them recently walked.

For 67 percent of the children who have them, warts disappear on their own within two or three years; and for 95 percent of the children, warts will be gone within 10 years. Still, some warts must be treated. Plantar warts usually require treatment because they cause pain. Warts that extend under the nails may produce permanent deformities if they are not treated. And warts on the face and eyelids are removed for cosmetic reasons. All other warts are harmless and can be ignored unless they are annoying, bleed frequently, or become infected.

DIAGNOSIS

Many warts are unmistakable, but some are not. When they are tiny, plantar warts may be mistaken for small brown splinters on the sole of the foot. They also may be indistinguishable when surrounded by a callus.

HOME TREATMENT

To safely remove warts (other than those on the face), use one of several commercial wart preparations. Usually, treatment must continue for many days or weeks.

PRECAUTIONS

● Do not treat any warts on the face or eyelids at home. ● If excessive pain or redness occurs on the surrounding skin, stop treatment. ● Plantar warts may be removed by home treatment, but the success rate is small. ● Warts that involve the cuticles or extend under the nails should not be treated at home.

DOCTOR'S TREATMENT

No treatment is successful in all cases. Treatment may even spread warts, or they may recur following treatment. In general, your doctor will remove warts with acids, podophyllin, electric cauterization, surgery (curetting), liquid nitrogen, solid carbon dioxide, or phenol.

Whooping Cough

DESCRIPTION

Whooping cough is the most misunderstood childhood illness today. It is a highly contagious infection of the respiratory tract.

In an unimmunized individual, whooping cough begins with a runny nose, low-grade fever (100°F oral or 101°F rectal), and a cough that gradually worsens over the next two to three weeks. Then, the cough becomes characteristic: It is worse at night than during the day and is paroxysmal (several coughs occur at once without inhalation in between). At the end of a spasm the child makes a "whoop" or strangling sound as air is sucked into the lungs; vomiting of thick mucus follows. The severe, strangling cough persists for another two to three weeks and gradually subsides in three to six more weeks. But the cough may return with new respiratory infections.

Whooping cough can be serious in infants under one year. As many as 40 percent of infants under five months of age die. Newborns are not immune.

DIAGNOSIS

The diagnosis may not be obvious, unless the child develops a "whoop."

The child who has been immunized may have full or partial immunity, but without boosters, the immunity declines over the years. A child who is partially immune may have a mild (aborted) case of whooping cough that produces none of whooping cough's identifiable characteristics. In the absence of characteristic symptoms, laboratory tests must confirm the diagnosis for most cases.

All the organisms that cause whooping cough are difficult to grow on cultures and more modern techniques for the isolation of these organisms are not readily available. Because it may be difficult to diagnose and both doctors and parents hold the misconception that the disease is rare, many of the cases of whooping cough are not detected or even suspected.

HOME TREATMENT

Cough suppressants may help, but no cough mixture is very effective. A child who has whooping cough should be isolated from young siblings.

PRECAUTIONS

● Infants should be immunized against whooping cough. They are not naturally immune to the disease, and the mortality rate among infants with whooping cough is high. ● If your child has been exposed to whooping cough check with your doctor. ● Adolescents and young adults whose immunity has weakened are also susceptible to whooping cough.

DOCTOR'S TREATMENT

Your doctor will try to establish a diagnosis with the help of a complete blood count and cultures of the nose and throat. Most often, however, the patient's history and the doctor's clinical judgment are all that are dependable. Your doctor may prescribe erythromycin for 10 to 14 days to counter contagiousness. If given early enough, it may shorten the course of the illness.

INDEX

A

A and D ointment,
  for diaper rash, 51
abdominal pain,
  with appendicitis, 19
  with colic, 35
  with hernia, 75
  with intestinal allergies, 88
  with mumps, 97
  with pinworms, 100
  with stomach ache, acute, 123
  with stomach ache, chronic, 125
  with strep throat, 126
  with swallowed objects, 132
  with torsion of testicle, 138
  with urinary tract infections, 146
abdominal swelling,
  in hernia, 75
abrasions, see scrapes
acetaminophen, 9, 10
  for appendicitis, 19
  for bronchitis, 27
  for chicken pox, 30
  for common cold, 37
  for dislocations, 121
  for earache, 57
  for gastroenteritis, acute, 64
  for growing pains, 65
  for hand, foot, and mouth disease,
    68
  for headache from concussion, 71
  for herpes simplex, 76
  for infectious mononucleosis, 82
  for influenza, 83
  for laryngitis, 91
  for measles, 94
  for mumps, 97
  for polio, 105
  for roseola, 110
  for rubella, 111
  for sinusitis, 116
  for sprains, 121
  for strep throat, 126
  for styes, 128
  for sunburn, 130
  for swimmer's ear, 134
  for teething, 136
alcohol,
  for swimmer's ear, 134
allergies, intestinal, 88

aluminum sulfate,
  for athlete's foot, 22
amblyopia ex anopsia, 92
aminophylline,
  for asthma, 21
anemia,
  and jaundice, 89
  with leukemia, 93
  with stomach ache, chronic, 125
animal bites, 18
antibiotic eye drops,
  for styes, 128
antibiotic ointment, 98
antibiotics, 17
  for athlete's foot, 22
  for bronchitis, 27
  for pneumonia, 101
  for puncture wounds, 107
  for sinusitis, 116
  for sore throat, 118
  for swimmer's ear, 134
  for tonsillitis, 144
  for urinary tract infections, 146
antihistamines,
  for asthma, 21
  for hand, foot, and mouth disease,
    68
  for hay fever, 70
  for hives, 78
  for insect bites, 86
  for nosebleeds, 98
  for poison ivy, 104
  for sunburn, 130
antirabies vaccine, 18
aphasia, 119
appendicitis, 19
  and pinworms, 100
appetite, loss of,
  with bronchitis, 27
  with mumps, 97
  with rubella, 111
  with teething, 136
arthritis,
  and strep throat, 126
aspirin, 9, 10
  and Reye's syndrome, 108
  for appendicitis, 19
  for bronchitis, 27
  for chicken pox, 30
  for earache, 57
  for growing pains, 65
  for headache from concussion, 71
  for headaches, 71
  for polio, 105
  for sunburn, 130
  for swimmer's ear, 134
  for teething, 136

asthma, 11, 20-21
in intestinal allergies, 88
astigmatism,
and lazy eye, 92
athlete's foot, 22, 109

B

backaches,
in urinary tract infections, 146
bacterial infections,
with hay fever, 70
bacterial pneumonia, 101
baking soda,
and tap-water paste, for sunburn,
130
bedwetting, 24
and urinary tract infections, 146
benzyl benzoate,
for head lice infestation, 73
beta-hemolytic streptococci, 126
bites, animal, 18
blistering,
in burns, 29
in hand, foot, and mouth disease, 68
in impetigo, 81
in poison ivy, 104
blisters, 25
in athlete's foot, 22
blood from ear canal,
in concussion, 39
blood from nose,
in concussion, 39
blood in stools,
in intestinal allergies, 88
in leukemia, 93
in stomach ache, chronic, 125
boils, 26
bone deformity,
in fractures, 62
bone pain,
in leukemia, 93
bowel movements, 53
characteristics of in infant
diarrhea, 54
brain damage,
with Reye's syndrome, 108
with speech problems, 119
breathing difficulty,
with concussion, 39
with epiglottitis, 46
breathing, rapid,
with dehydration, 50
breathing, slow,
with dehydration, 50
bronchitis, 27

bruises, 28
and leukemia, 93
burn ointments,
for sunburn, 130
burns, 29
prevention of, 29

C

calamine lotion,
for hives, 78
for insect bites, 86
for poison ivy, 104
calcium acetate,
for athlete's foot, 22
canker sores,
with herpes simplex, 76
carbuncle, 26
cataracts,
and lazy eye, 92
Center for Disease Control, 18
chewing on fingers,
with teething, 136
chicken pox, 30-31
and Reye's syndrome, 108
chills,
with influenza, 83
choking, 32-34
first aid treatment for, 32
versus gagging, 32
clamminess,
with fainting, 61
Clostridium tetani germ, 142
clumsiness,
with hyperactivity, 79
cocoa butter,
for sunburn, 130
codeine,
for polio, 105
cold applications,
for bruises, 28
for burns, 29
colic, 35-36
Colorado tick fever, 86
coma,
with Reye's syndrome, 108
common colds, 37-38
when to call pediatrician, 16
common wart, 150
compresses, cold water,
for sunburn, 130
concussion, 39
confusion,
with concussion, 39
with Reye's syndrome, 108

153

conjunctivitis, 40
constipation, 41
  with stomach ache, chronic, 125
convulsions,
  with chicken pox, 30
  with meningitis, 95
  with Reye's syndrome, 108
  with roseola, 110
  with tetanus, 142
convulsive movements,
   with fainting, 61
coughing, 12, 43
  when to call pediatrician, 16
  with asthma, 20
  with bronchitis, 27
  with common colds, 37
  with influenza, 83
  with laryngitis, 91
  with measles, 94
  with pneumonia, 101
  with sinusitis, 116
  with whooping cough, 151
cough looseners, 43
cough medicines, 10,11
  for measles, 94
  uses of, 43
cough suppressants, 43
cough tighteners, 43
cracking between the toes,
  in athlete's foot, 22
cradle cap, 44
cramps,
  with gastroenteritis, acute, 64
Crohn's disease, 53
crossed eyes, 45
croup, 11, 46-47
  types of, 46
curvature of the spine, 112
cuts, 48
cystitis,
  and pinworms, 100
cysts,
  versus styes, 128

D

deafness, 49
  and mumps, 97
  and rubella, 111
  and speech problems, 119
decongestants, 10
  for hay fever, 70
  for hives, 78
  for nosebleeds, 98
  for sinusitis, 116
deformity,
  with sprains and dislocations, 121

dehydration, 50
  with diarrhea, 53
  with diarrhea in infants, 54
  with gastroenteritis, acute, 64
Desitin ointment,
  for diaper rash, 51
diaper rashes, 51-52
diarrhea, 53-54
  in appendicitis, 19
  in children, 53
  in infants, 54
  in influenza, 83
  in intestinal allergies, 88
  in stomach ache, chronic, 125
  when to call pediatrician, 16
diarrhea, chronic,
  and teething, 136
  in gastroenteritis, acute, 64
diminished hearing,
  with earache, 57
diphtheria, 14, 46, 55
diphtheria, tetanus, whooping cough
  vaccine, 14
discharge from ear,
  in swimmer's ear, 134
diseases requiring immunizations,
  14-15
dislocated elbow, 56
disorientation,
  in encephalitis, 59
draining ear,
  as a complication of earache, 57
drooling,
  with teething, 136
drowsiness,
  in concussion, 39
  in dehydration, 50
dryness of the mouth,
  in dehydration, 50
DTP vaccine, see diphtheria, tetanus,
  and whooping cough vaccine

E

earaches, 12, 57-58
  in common colds, 37
  in hay fever, 70
  when to call pediatrician, 16
ear canal problems, 49
eardrum and middle ear problems, 49
ear infections, 16
ear injury, 57
earplugs,
  for swimmer's ear, 134
earwax, impacted, 57
eczema,
  with intestinal allergies, 88

eighth cranial nerve problems, 49
elbow, dislocated, 56
emetic, 11
emotional outburst,
  in hyperactivity, 79
emotional stress,
  with stomach ache, chronic, 125
emotions,
  and asthma, 20
encephalitis, 15, 59
  and chicken pox, 30
  and measles, 94
  and Reye's syndrome, 108
enema,
  for appendicitis, 19
  for constipation, 41
enuresis, see bedwetting
ephedrine,
  for asthma, 21
epiglottitis, 46
epinephrine,
  for insect bites, 86
Epsom salt solution,
  for blisters, 25
  for boils, 26
  for puncture wounds, 107
erythema multiforme, 78
erythroblastosis fetalis, 90
erythromycin,
  for diphtheria, 55
Escherichia coli bacillus, 146
expectorant cough remedy,
  for laryngitis, 91
eye drops, antibiotic,
  for styes, 128
eye injuries, 60
eyes not parallel,
  in concussion, 39

F

failure to thrive,
  in intestinal allergies, 88
fainting, 61
farsightedness,
  and lazy eye, 92
fatigue,
  with hay fever, 70
  with influenza, 83
  with pneumonia, 101
femoral hernia, 75
fever, 8-9, 10, 12
  treatment of, 9
  when to call pediatrician, 16
  with appendicitis, 19
  with bronchitis, 27
  with chicken pox, 30

with common colds, 37
with dehydration, 50
with diarrhea in infants, 54
with earaches, 57
with encephalitis, 59
with epiglottitis, 46
with gastroenteritis, acute, 64
with hand, foot, and mouth disease,
  68
with hay fever, 70
with herpes simplex, 76
with infectious mononucleosis, 82
with influenza, 83
with laryngitis, 91
with measles, 94
with meningitis, 95
with mumps, 97
with pneumonia, 101
with polio, 105
with roseola, 110
with rubella, 111
with stomach ache, chronic, 125
with strep throat, 126
with sunburn, 130
with swallowed objects, 132
with swimmer's ear, 134
with torsion of testicle, 138
with tonsillitis, 144
with urinary tract infections, 146
with whooping cough, 151
fever blisters,
  with herpes simplex, 76
flushing of the face,
  with influenza, 83
fractures, 62-63
fright,
  with fainting, 61
fungicidal ointments,
  for athlete's foot, 22
furunculosis, 26

G

gagging,
  versus choking, 32
gamma-benzene hexachloride,
  for head lice infestation, 73
gastroenteritis, acute, 64
German measles, 111
  with jaundice, 90
glucose,
  and Reye's syndrome, 108
glycerine,
  for swimmer's ear, 134
growing pains, 65
gum boils, 76
gynecomastia, 66

H

hand, foot, and mouth disease, 68
hay fever, 11, 70
headache, 71-72
  when to call pediatrician, 16
  with chicken pox, 30
  with concussion, 39
  with encephalitis, 59
  with hay fever, 70
  with hypertension, 71
  with influenza, 83
  with meningitis, 95
  with migraine, 71
  with mumps, 97
  with pneumonia, 101
  with strep throat, 126
head cold,
  with earaches, 57
head lice, 73
heat rash, 74
hernia, 75
herpes simplex, 76-77
hives, 11, 78
  versus sunburn, 130
  with intestinal allergies, 88
hoarseness,
  with laryngitis, 91
hyperactivity, 79-80
  with Reye's syndrome, 108
hyperkinesis, see hyperactivity

I

imipramine,
  for bedwetting, 24
immunizations, 14-15
  against diphtheria, 55
  against Hemophilus influenzae, 14
  against measles, 15
  against mumps, 97
  against polio, 15
  against rubella, 111
  against tetanus, 142
  against whooping cough, 151
  reaction to, 59
impacted earwax, 57
impetigo, 81
infantile paralysis, 105
infection,
  and puncture wounds, 106
  and scoliosis, 112
infectious mononucleosis, 82
influenza, 83-84
  and Reye's syndrome, 108
influenza virus, 84
ingrown toenails, 85

injury,
  and scoliosis, 112
inner ear problems, 49
insect bites, 11, 86
  types of, 86
intestinal allergies, 88
irritants,
  and asthma, 20
itching,
  with athlete's foot, 22
  with hand, foot, and mouth disease,
    68
  with hay fever, 70
  with head lice infestation, 73
  with heat rash, 74
  with hives, 78
  with pinworms, 100
  with poison ivy, 104

J

jaundice, 89-90
  in children, 89
  in newborns, 90
juvenile wart, 150

K

Kaolin
  for diarrhea, 53
Koplik's spots, 94

L

lacerations (cuts), 48
lack of concentration,
  in hyperactivity, 79
lactase deficiency,
  with stomach ache, chronic, 125
laryngitis, 91
larynx abnormalities,
  with speech problems, 119
laxative,
  for appendicitis, 19
lazy eye, 45, 92
learning disabilities,
  in hyperactivity, 79
leukemia, 8, 93
light-headedness,
  with fainting, 61
lip abnormalities,
  with speech problems, 119
liver damage,
  with Reye's syndrome, 108
liver enlargement, 93
lockjaw, see tetanus
loss of consciousness, see fainting

loss of elasticity of the skin,
  in dehydration, 50
loss of function,
  with sprains and dislocations, 121
low blood sugar,
  with fainting, 61
  with Reye's syndrome, 108
lubricant, 10
lymph node, enlargement,
  with common cold, 37
  with diphtheria, 55
  with earache, 57
  with head lice infestation, 73
  with infectious mononucleosis, 82
  with leukemia, 93
  with roseola, 110
  with rubella, 111
  with strep throat, 126
  with swimmer's ear, 134
  with tonsillitis, 144

M

malaise,
  with bronchitis, 27
  with infectious mononucleosis, 82
  with polio, 105
mastoiditis,
  as a complication of earaches, 57
measles, 94
measles, mumps, rubella vaccine, 15
medications, 10-11, 12-13
  dosage, 12
  duration of, 12
  for infants, 12
  for older children, 13
  timing, 12
medicine chest, pediatric, 10-11
  recommended contents, 10
memory loss,
  with concussion, 39
meningitis, 95
  as a complication of earache, 57
meningococcus, 95
mental retardation,
  and speech problems, 119
merthiolate antiseptic,
  for puncture wounds, 106
metaproterenol,
  for asthma, 21
middle ear infection,
  and strep throat, 126
miliaria, see heat rash
minimal brain dysfunction, 79
MMR vaccine, see measles, mumps,
  rubella vaccine
motion sickness, 96

mumps, 97
muscle aches,
  with influenza, 83
  with polio, 105
muscle spasms,
  with asthma, 20
  with tetanus, 142
muscle weakness,
  and scoliosis, 112

N

narrowing of visual fields,
  with fainting, 61
nasal congestion,
  with bronchitis, 27
  with common colds, 37
  with hay fever, 70
nasal discharge,
  with bronchitis, 27
  with common colds, 37
  with hay fever, 70
nausea,
  with fainting, 61
  with motion sickness, 96
  with polio, 105
  with torsion of testicle, 138
nephritis,
  and strep throat, 126
nose abnormalities,
  with speech problems, 119
nosebleeds, 98
  in leukemia, 93
nose infection,
  in diphtheria, 55

O

orchitis, 138

P

pain,
  with boils, 26
  with conjunctivitis, 40
  with earache, 57
  with fainting, 61
  with fractures, 62
  with ingrown toenails, 85
  with sinusitis, 116
  with styes, 128
  with swimmer's ear, 134
  with tonsillitis, 144
paleness,
  in leukemia, 93
paralysis,
  in polio, 105

parent/physician partnership, 6-7
patches, crusted,
  in cradle cap, 44
patches, scaly,
  in cradle cap, 44
patches, yellowish,
  in cradle cap, 44
pectin,
  for diarrhea, 53
pediatrician,
  how to choose, 6
  when to call,
    about common cold, 16
    about cough, 16
    about diarrhea, 16
    about earache, 16
    about fever, 16
    about headache, 16
    about sore throat, 16
    about stomach ache, 16
    about vomiting, 16
pediatric medicine chest, 10
penicillin,
  for diphtheria, 55
  for impetigo, 81
  for strep throat, 127
perforated ear,
  as a complication of earache, 57
peritonsillar abscess, 144
pertussis, see whooping cough
petechiae, 28
  with gastroenteritis, acute, 64
  with meningitis, 95
petroleum jelly,
  for diaper rash, 51
  for nosebleeds, 98
physical exertion,
  and asthma, 20
physical fatigue,
  with fainting, 61
pigeon toes, 99
pinworms, 100
plantar warts, 150
pneumonia, 101
  and measles, 94
  and strep throat, 126
Poison Control Center, 11
poisoning, 102-103
  and encephalitis, 59
poison ivy, 11, 104
  versus sunburn, 130
polio, 15, 105
poliomyelitis, 105
potassium iodine,
  for asthma, 21
potassium permanganate,
  for athlete's foot, 22

prostration,
  in chicken pox, 30
  in meningitis, 95
  in strep throat, 126
  with sunburn, 130
pseudogynecomastia, 66
pulse, slow,
  with concussion, 39
puncture wound, 106
pupils of different size,
  with concussion, 39
pus,
  in boils, 26
  in conjunctivitis, 40
  in cuts, 48

Q

quinsy sore throat, 144

R

rabies vaccine, 18
radiation therapy,
  and scoliosis, 112
rashes,
  diaper, 51
  heat, 74
  poison ivy, 104
  with chicken pox, 30
  with hand, foot, and mouth disease,
    68
  with head lice infestation, 73
  with infectious mononucleosis, 82
  with measles, 94
  with roseola, 110
  with rubella, 111
reaction,
  to rubella vaccine, 15
redness of eyes,
  with common colds, 37
  with influenza, 83
  with measles, 94
  with sinusitis, 116
redness of skin,
  with boils, 26
  with burns, 29
  with diaper rash, 51
  with heat rash, 74
  with hives, 78
  with ingrown toenails, 85
  with poison ivy, 104
  with rubella, 111
red streaks,
  with cuts, 48
Reye's syndrome, 10, 30, 108
  and aspirin, 108

rheumatic fever,
   and strep throat, 126
rickettsialpox, 86
ringworm, 109
roseola, 110
rubella, 111
rubeola, 94
runny nose,
   with intestinal allergies, 88
   with measles, 94
   with roseola, 110
   with whooping cough, 151

S

Sabin vaccine, 15
Salk vaccine, 105
scaling of skin,
   with athlete's foot, 109
   with diaper rash, 51
   with ringworm, 109
scarlatina, 126
scarlet fever, 126
scoliosis, 112
scorching,
   with burns, 29
scrapes, 106, 114
scratchy throat,
   with bronchitis, 27
   with common colds, 37
   with laryngitis, 91
sepsis,
   with jaundice, 90
shortness of breath,
   in asthma, 20
sinusitis, 116
   and conjunctivitis, 40
   and strep throat, 126
sleepiness, abnormal,
   with Reye's syndrome, 108
sneezing,
   with common colds, 37
   with hay fever, 70
sodium perborate,
   for herpes simplex, 76
sore throat, 118
   and conjunctivitis, 40
   when to call pediatrician, 16
   with common colds, 37
   with infectious mononucleosis, 82
   with influenza, 83
   with polio, 105
   with strep throat, 126
   with tonsillitis, 144
sores in the mouth,
   in hand, foot, and mouth disease, 68

   in herpes simplex, 76
spasmodic croup, 46
speech problems, 119-120
spleen enlargement, 93
spotted throat
   with strep throat, 126
sprains, 121
staphylococcal infection,
   with impetigo, 81
   with pneumonia, 101
   with styes, 128
staphylococcus aureus, 26
steroids, 10, 11
   for asthma, 21
   for diphtheria, 55
   for hives, 78
   for insect bites, 86
   for sunburn, 130
stiff neck,
   with concussion, 39
   with meningitis, 95
   with polio, 105
stomach ache, acute, 123-124
   when to call pediatrician, 16
stomache ache, chronic, 125
strep infections, 12
strep throat, 8, 126-127
streptococcal infection,
   in impetigo, 81
stuttering, 119-120
styes, 26, 128
sunburn, 130
sunken eyes,
   in dehydration, 50
sun poisoning, 11
sunscreens, choice of, 130
swallowed objects, 132
swallowing difficulty,
   in epiglottitis, 46
swelling,
   in cuts, 48
   in poison ivy, 104
   of gums, 76, 93
   of hand, 56
   of salivary glands, 97
   of wrist, 56
swimmer's ear, 134

T

teething, 136
temperature,
   how to take, 9
   oral, 9
   rectal, 9

testicle, torsion of, 138
testicle, undescended, 140
tetanus, 14, 142
tetanus immunization, 14
  for cuts, 48
  for puncture wounds, 106
  for scrapes, 114
theophylline,
  for asthma, 21
thermometers, 9, 10, 11
  care of, 9
tinea capitis, 109
tinea corporis, 109
tinea pedis, 109
tiredness,
  with leukemia, 93
tongue abnormalities,
  with speech problems, 119
tonsillitis, 144
  and conjunctivitis, 40
torsion of testicle, 138
tracheostomy,
  for diphtheria, 55
tripod sign,
  in encephalitis, 59
  in meningitis, 95
  in polio, 105
tularemia, 86
tumor, of adrenal glands,
  in gynecomastia, 66
tumor, of testes,
  in gynecomastia, 66
tumors,
  and scoliosis, 112
typhus, 86

U

ulcers,
  of the mouth, 76
umbilical hernia, 75
unconsciousness,
  in fainting, 61
  with concussion, 39
undecylenate,
  for athlete's foot, 22
undecylenic acid,
  for athlete's foot, 22
upper respiratory infections,
  and asthma, 20
urinary tract infections, 146
urine, discoloration,
  with urinary tract infections, 146
urine, foul-smelling
  with urinary tract infections, 146
urination, frequent,
  with urinary tract infections, 146

urination, infrequent,
  with dehydration, 50
urination, painful,
  with appendicitis, 19
  with stomach ache, chronic, 123
  with urinary tract infections, 146
urticaria, 78

V

vaccine, 14-15
ventral hernia, 75
vermifuges (worm medicines), 100
viral infection,
  and Reye's syndrome, 108
viral pneumonia, 101
vitamin A and D ointment,
  for diaper rash, 51
vomiting, 148-149
  when to call pediatrician, 16
  with chicken pox, 30
  with dehydration, 50
  with diarrhea, 53
  with diarrhea in infants, 54
  with encephalitis, 59
  with gastroenteritis, acute, 64
  with influenza, 83
  with intestinal allergies, 88
  with meningitis, 95
  with motion sickness, 96
  with Reye's syndrome, 108
  with stomach ache, chronic, 125
  with swallowed objects, 132
  with torsion of testicle, 138
  with urinary tract infections, 146

W

warm applications,
  for bruises, 28
warts, 150
watery eyes,
  with common colds, 37
weakness,
  in influenza, 83
  in leukemia, 93
weight loss,
  with diarrhea in infants, 54
whooping cough (pertussis), 14, 151
worm medicines, see vermifuges

Z

zinc oxide,
  for diaper rash, 51